This Book Belongs to

. . . .

S'mores in a Jar,
page 145

Gifts from the Kitchen

Oxmoor House®

Gifts *from the* Kitchen

©2014 by Gooseberry Patch
2545 Farmers Dr., #380, Columbus, Ohio 43235
1-800-854-6673, **gooseberrypatch.com**
©2014 by Time Home Entertainment Inc.
135 West 50th Street, New York, NY 10020

ISBN-13: 978-0-8487-4355-0
ISBN-10: 0-8487-4355-5
Library of Congress Control Number: 2012943238
Printed in the United States of America
Second Printing 2014

Oxmoor House
Editorial Director: Leah McLaughlin
Creative Director: Felicity Keane
Brand Manager: Vanessa Tiongson
Senior Editor: Rebecca Brennan
Managing Editor: Rebecca Benton

Gooseberry Patch Gifts from the Kitchen
Editor: Natalie Kelly Brown
Senior Designer: Melissa Clark
Director, Test Kitchen: Elizabeth Tyler Austin
Assistant Directors, Test Kitchen: Julie Christopher, Julie Gunter
Recipe Developers and Testers: Wendy Ball, R.D., Victoria E. Cox, Stefanie Maloney, Callie Nash, Leah Van Deren
Recipe Editor: Alyson Moreland Haynes
Food Stylists: Margaret Monroe Dickey, Catherine Crowell Steele
Photography Director: Jim Bathie
Senior Photo Stylist: Kay E. Clarke
Photo Stylist: Katherine Eckert Coyne
Assistant Photo Stylist: Mary Louise Menendez
Assistant Production Manager: Diane Rose

Contributors
Project Editor: Perri Hubbard
Recipe Developers and Testers: Tamara Goldis, Erica Hopper, Tonya Johnson, Kyra Moncrief, Kathleen Royal Phillips
Copy Editor: Dolores Hydock
Proofreader: Norma Butterworth-McKittrick
Indexer: Nanette Cardon
Interns: Erin Bishop, Maribeth Browning, Mackenzie Cogle, Laura Hoxworth, Alicia Lavender, Alison Loughman, Anna Pollock, Ashley White
Food Stylist: Ana Price Kelley
Photographers: Beau Gustafson, Beth Dreiling Hontzas, Becky Luigart-Stayner
Photo Stylist: Missie Crawford, Caitlin Van Horn

Time Home Entertainment Inc.
Publisher: Jim Childs
VP, Strategy & Business Development: Steven Sandonato
Executive Director, Marketing Services: Carol Pittard
Executive Director, Retail & Special Sales: Tom Mifsud
Director, Bookazine Development & Marketing: Laura Adam
Executive Publishing Director: Joy Butts
Finance Director: Glenn Buonocore
Associate General Counsel: Helen Wan

To order additional publications, call 1-800-765-6400.
For more books to enrich your life, visit **oxmoorhouse.com**
To search, savor, and share thousands of recipes, visit **myrecipes.com**

Cover: Orange Puff Cupcakes (page 87)

Sour Cream-Apple Pie,
page 99

Cool Mint
Chocolate
Swirls,
page 33

Kielbasa-Cabbage Soup,
page 130

contents

Greetings from Jo Ann & Vickie 7

The Giving Kitchen 8

Christmas Cookie Swap.................. 16

Yummy Brownies & Bars................ 40

Old-Fashioned Candies.................. 60

Blue-Ribbon Cakes & Pies 76

Cheery Sips & Stirs 100

Best-Ever Muffins & Breads 108

Cozy Soups & More...................... 124

Easy Treats in a Twinkle 142

Metric Equivalents Chart 156

Index 157

Project Index 159

Our Story 160

Zippy Pepper Jelly, page 152

Dear Friend,

Whatever the occasion or season, any one of the special treats found throughout these pages will bring a warm smile to family & friends. From easy packaging ideas to treasured recipes perfect for sharing, we have what you're looking for and more. With simple ingredients, our yummy collection of family favorites also includes many reader tips and memories to enjoy. We recommend that you keep your gift-wrapping essentials in one spot so there's no rummaging through closets and drawers looking for paper, ribbon or tape.

If you love cookies with a soft, cake-like texture, then Cherry Cardamom Cookies (page 27) are the ones for you. These unique little gems have just the right amount of spice and sweetness, and make for a pretty presentation in a lidded jar wrapped with decorative paper and tied with a festive ribbon. Sweet Raspberry-Oat Bars (page 54), full of buttery and crumbly goodness layered with raspberry jam, are the perfect bake-and-take treat.

For a unique twist on classic eggnog, serve Chocolate Eggnog (page 102). This rich, chocolatey beverage topped with sweetened whipped cream and a fine dusting of cocoa is sure to be a huge hit during the holidays. Have someone in need of a little comfort? Bring them a container of Herbed Chicken-Barley Soup (page 128). The healthy addition of barley instead of traditional noodles will be a welcome change for a go-to dish.

We hope these time-honored recipes and fun gift-packaging ideas will reward you with accolades for years to come.

From our families to yours,

JoAnn & Vickie

The Giving Kitchen

Surprise a special someone with these clever packaging ideas for those last-minute gift-wrapping projects. Don't miss out on handy storage solutions and tips on how to get organized.

gift wrap corner

We found it's best to keep all craft and gifting supplies in one place. Store items in a closet or on a bookshelf. This keeps clutter to a minimum and you won't have to search through drawers and boxes for those last-minute gift ideas. Here are a few items you'll definitely want to keep on hand.

Decorative paper towel holder A handy way to store spools of ribbon
Twine
Paper and plastic drinking straws Use them to glue labels with recipe names or fun sayings onto straws and insert them into party treats.
Scrapbook paper
Cardboard boxes Purchase ones with labels on the side
Wrapping paper
Large glass cookie jar Great storage for ribbon
Vintage bread baskets Look for them at yard sales and antique markets
Buttons Store in a glass jar with lid for easy access
Cupcake liners Keep on hand a variety of sizes, colors and patterns
Wooden or paper berry baskets Line with colorful tissue paper, linens or a tea towel
Vintage cookie tins
Canning jars

CD Holders

Paper CD holders in a variety of colors
Assorted large homemade cookies
Gift tags

The open window on a CD holder makes for perfect cookie packaging, and is a fun way to pass out the class valentines. Slide the cookies, front side up, into the CD holders and attach a ribbon and a valentine tag.

Coffee Mugs

Vintage coffee mugs
Biscotti or homemade goodies
Brown craft paper tags
Felt pieces

Thank friends or neighbors by giving them a vintage coffee mug filled with an assortment of biscotti or other homemade treats. A collection of unique coffee mugs can be a great conversation starter. Stamp or hand-write a greeting and attach it to a colorful felt piece found at your local craft store.

Burlap and Buttons

10"x10" pieces of burlap
Wired ribbon
Buttons in different shapes, colors
　　and sizes
Small plastic zipping bags
Packaged snacks

　　Surprise loved ones with their own snack bag. Cut burlap squares and fray to about one inch from the edge. Place your favorite snacks in plastic zipping bags; tie the burlap around the bags using wired ribbon. String on the buttons, add a tag and you are ready for a sleepover, picnic or a long car ride to grandma's house.

Brown Lunch Bags

Brown lunch bags
Doilies in assorted shapes and sizes
Variety of 1-yd. lengths of ribbon
Hole punch
Decorative-edged scissors
Craft glue

　　Here's a simple birthday gift wrap idea that won't require a trip to the store. A brown lunch bag makes one of the easiest gift-wrapping essentials and almost everyone should have some on hand. Create a one-of-a-kind gift bag with this inexpensive household item. All you'll need is a hole punch and an assortment of ribbons…it's as easy as that! Personalize them by using craft glue to attach doilies to bags.

Wide-Mouth Jars

Wide-mouth jars with lids
Wrapping paper scraps
Craft paper tags
Twine or narrow ribbon
Dried peppers

A wide-mouth jar can never have too many uses. Package a spicy chutney or homemade sauce to hand to guests as a take-away at your next garden club party. Simply pour sauce into jar, add the center part of the top only, attach a 5"x5" piece of colorful wrapping paper to the top and screw the rim onto the wide-mouth jar. Tag it with a fun message and a colorful pepper and it is ready to give!

Ice-Cream Party Favors

Tissue paper in assorted colors
Sugar ice-cream cones
Variety of candy
Party favors

A clever idea for an ice-cream social is to fill sugar cones with various candies or gumballs. Stack the candy-filled cones upright in a container with assorted party favors. Guests will be able to customize their own ice-cream treats!

Tea Towels

Parchment paper
Vintage tea towels
Twine
Mini bread loaves

Don't know what to do with
all of those vintage linens, fabrics,
tablecloths and towels in the linen
closet? Monogram the initials of a
friend or family member at the end
of a tea towel and use it as a gift wrap
for a mini bread loaf. Wrap the loaf
in parchment paper, fold the linen to
fit over the loaf and tie with bright
twine and a tag. What a way to say
welcome to the neighborhood or as a
just-because.

Basket

Vintage baskets
Homemade soup
Paper products
Tea towels
Assorted crackers and
      plastic zipping bags

A variety of wooden or straw
baskets can go a long way when you
fill them with items from your pantry.
Attach the recipe to a jar of soup along
with stackable soup bowls with tops,
wooden spoons, assorted crackers,
brightly colored disposable napkins
and a great book.

Aprons

Cleaning supplies
Small scrub brush
Vintage hand towel or tablecloth
Kitchen apron
Enamel bucket
Cleaning gloves

Home cleaning products are an ideal gift idea for a couple's bridal shower or if you have a friend or neighbor going through home renovations. Arrange the cleaning essentials in the bucket and dress up an apron with an appliqué from an old tea towel or tablecloth. Use a seam ripper to remove the appliqué and then sew onto apron pocket by using the zigzag stitch on your sewing machine.

Aluminum Cans

Aluminum cans
Wrapping paper
Craft glue
Clothespins
Easter grass
Glass salad dressing jars

Give a holiday gift from the kitchen that includes your favorite salad dressing recipe. Remove the label from a clean, large aluminum can, cut wrapping paper to size and glue paper onto the back of the can. Add Easter grass to the can and place the jar of salad dressing inside. Attach a gift tag with a clothespin and ornament...how simple!

White Chocolate Cookies, page 23
Almond Cream Spritz, page 21
Butterscotch Gingerbread Cookies, page 29
Christmas Peppermint &
    Chocolate Meringues, page 39

Christmas Cookie Swap

Take home a variety of cherished recipes...get ready for smiles of delight at a merry gathering of bake & swap.

delight your hostess!

Fill a pretty drinking glass with Dazzling Neapolitan Cookies, cover the top with a dainty handkerchief and secure with a ribbon...a thoughtful hostess gift.

Dazzling Neapolitan Cookies

These cookies only look difficult...they're really easy to make!

1 c. butter, softened
1 c. sugar
1 egg
1 t. vanilla extract
2 ½ c. all-purpose flour
1 ½ t. baking powder
½ t. salt

1-oz. sq. baking chocolate, melted
⅓ c. chopped pecans
¼ c. chopped candied cherries, diced
2 drops red food coloring
⅓ c. flaked coconut
½ t. almond extract

In a large bowl, combine butter and sugar. Beat with an electric mixer at medium speed until light and fluffy; add egg and vanilla, beating until blended. Gradually beat in flour, baking powder and salt. Divide dough into thirds and place each third in a separate bowl. Stir chocolate and pecans into one third, cherries and food coloring into another third and coconut and almond extract into remaining third.

Line an 8"x8" baking pan with plastic wrap, allowing 2 to 4 inches to extend over sides; press chocolate mixture evenly into bottom of pan. Add coconut mixture and then cherry mixture, gently pressing each layer; cover and chill 8 hours. Using plastic wrap as handles, lift dough from pan; cut into 5 equal sections. Carefully cut each section into ⅛ inch-thick slices; place on ungreased baking sheets. Bake at 375 degrees for 8 to 10 minutes, until golden; remove to wire racks to cool. Store in an airtight container. Makes 8 dozen.

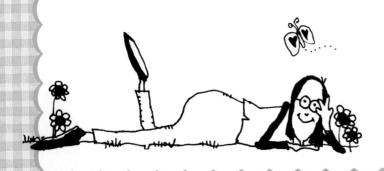

Almond Cream Spritz

Almond Cream Spritz

pictured on page 16

1 c. butter, softened
3-oz. pkg. cream cheese, softened
½ c. sugar
½ t. almond extract
¼ t. vanilla extract
2 c. all-purpose flour
½ c. almonds, finely chopped

These tender cookies taste buttery with a delicate almond flavor.

In a large bowl, combine butter and cream cheese. Beat with an electric mixer at medium speed until well blended. Add sugar and extracts; beat well. Stir in flour. Cover and chill dough 30 minutes, or until easy to handle. Place dough in a cookie press and press out cookies onto ungreased baking sheets; sprinkle with almonds. Bake at 375 degrees for 8 to 10 minutes, until edges are lightly golden; remove to wire racks to cool (be sure to let pans cool between batches…a warm pan will cause dough to soften and spread). Store in an airtight container. Makes 5 dozen.

Lisa Johnson
Hallsville, TX

Orangey-Ginger Cookie Sticks

⅔ c. almonds
1 ¾ c. cake flour
2 t. ground ginger
1 t. baking powder
1 c. butter, softened
1 c. brown sugar, packed
6 T. plus 2 t. sugar, divided
2 T. orange zest
2 egg yolks, divided and beaten
½ t. vanilla extract
⅔ c. pistachios, finely chopped

If you prefer a less crunchy cookie, omit the third bake time.

Combine almonds, cake flour, ginger and baking powder in a food processor; process until finely ground. Combine butter, brown sugar and 6 tablespoons sugar in a large bowl. Beat with an electric mixer at medium speed until light and fluffy. Add zest, one egg yolk and vanilla; beat well. Add ground almond mixture, stirring just until blended. Stir in pistachios. Divide dough in half. Using floured hands, roll each half into a ½-inch-thick log on a lightly floured surface. Place logs 4 inches apart on a greased and floured baking sheet. Cover with plastic wrap and chill one hour. Brush logs with remaining egg yolk; sprinkle with remaining 2 teaspoons sugar.

Bake at 350 degrees for 30 minutes, or until deep golden and firm to the touch; cool 10 minutes. Using a serrated knife, cut logs crosswise into ½-inch-thick slices. Place sliced-side down on same baking sheet. Bake at 300 degrees for 12 minutes, or until golden. Turn over; bake an additional 12 minutes, or until golden. Remove to wire racks to cool completely. Store in an airtight container. Makes 1 ½ dozen.

Carrie O'Shea
Marina Del Ray, CA

Cookie exchanges are even more fun when guests bring copies of their recipes for sharing. As a special holiday surprise, make a cookie cookbook and give a copy to each guest. What a nice way to remember all of the festivities during a blustery January!

Espresso Bean Cookies

You can find chocolate-covered coffee beans in various package sizes at most coffee shops. One 6-ounce package equals about one cup.

1 c. butter, softened
¾ c. brown sugar, packed
¼ c. sugar
2 eggs
1 t. vanilla extract
2 ¼ c. all-purpose flour
1 t. baking soda

1 t. salt
½ t. cinnamon
1 c. chopped almonds, toasted
1 c. chocolate-covered coffee beans
4 1.4-oz. toffee candy bars, chopped

In a large bowl, beat butter with an electric mixer at medium speed until creamy. Gradually add sugars, beating well after each addition. Add eggs, one at a time, beating until blended after each addition; add vanilla, and beat until blended. In a separate bowl, combine flour, baking soda, salt and cinnamon. Gradually add flour mixture to butter mixture, beating well. Stir in almonds, coffee beans and chopped candy. Cover and chill dough until firm. Drop by teaspoonfuls onto ungreased baking sheets. Bake at 350 degrees for 10 to 11 minutes, until golden. Cool on pans one minute; remove to wire racks to cool completely. Store in an airtight container. Makes 4 dozen.

Kathy Grashoff
Fort Wayne, IN

White Chocolate Cookies

pictured on page 16

1 c. butter, softened
¾ c. brown sugar, packed
½ c. sugar
1 egg
½ t. almond extract
2 c. all-purpose flour
1 t. baking soda

¼ t. cinnamon
¼ t. ground ginger
¼ t. salt
6-oz. pkg. white baking
    chocolate, chopped
1 ½ c. chopped pecans

Ginger and almond extract give these special cookies their unique taste.

In a large bowl, beat butter and sugars with an electric mixer at medium speed until smooth. Add egg and extract; beat well. In a separate bowl, combine flour, baking soda, cinnamon, ginger and salt, stirring to mix; add flour mixture to butter mixture, stirring well. Blend in chocolate and pecans. Drop by teaspoonfuls 2 inches apart onto greased baking sheets. Bake at 350 degrees for 10 to 12 minutes, until lightly golden. Remove to wire racks to cool. Store in an airtight container. Makes 5 dozen.

Bunny Palmertree
Carrollton, MS

Lacy Florentine Cookies

¾ c. quick-cooking oats,
    uncooked
¾ c. all-purpose flour
¾ c. sugar
1 t. cinnamon
½ t. baking soda
½ t. salt

1 ½ c. sliced almonds
½ c. plus 2 T. butter, melted
¼ c. half-and-half
¼ c. light corn syrup
1 t. vanilla extract
4 1-oz. sqs. semi-sweet baking
    chocolate, melted

Sweet, buttery cookies...just like my Italian grandmother used to make.
—Regina

In a large bowl, combine oats, flour, sugar, cinnamon, baking soda and salt, stirring to mix; add almonds and stir well. Add butter, half-and-half, corn syrup and vanilla, stirring until well blended. Drop by tablespoonfuls 3 inches apart onto aluminum foil-lined, greased baking sheets, with 6 cookies per sheet. Bake one pan at a time at 350 degrees on center rack for 7 to 9 minutes, until edges are golden. Cool in pans 5 minutes; remove to wire racks to cool completely. Drizzle melted chocolate over cooled cookies. Store in an airtight container. Makes 4 dozen.

Regina Vining
Warwick, RI

Maple Sugar Cookies

For the best flavor, use pure maple syrup.

1 c. butter, softened
1 ¼ c. sugar
2 eggs
¼ c. maple syrup
1 T. vanilla extract

3 c. all-purpose flour
¾ t. baking powder
½ t. baking soda
½ t. salt

In a large bowl, beat butter and sugar with an electric mixer at medium speed until creamy. Add eggs, one at a time, beating well after each addition. Beat in syrup and vanilla. In a separate bowl, combine flour, baking powder, baking soda and salt, stirring to mix; gradually add flour mixture to butter mixture, stirring until blended. Cover and chill 2 hours. On a lightly floured surface, roll dough to ⅛-inch thickness; cut with a 2 ½-inch cookie cutter dipped in flour. Place cookies one inch apart on ungreased baking sheets. Bake at 350 degrees for 8 to 10 minutes, until golden. Remove to wire racks to cool completely. Store in an airtight container. Makes 3 dozen.

Michelle Crabtree
Lee's Summit, MO

a clever tip

Take two gift bags the same size but different colors and cut through the middle of each. Swap halves and glue together, overlapping edges by ½ inch. Glue a strip of wide ribbon around each bag to hide the seam... you'll have two clever boutique bags for giving cookies!

Maple Sugar Cookies

Cherry Cardamom Cookies

Quick Fruitcake Bites

2 c. mini marshmallows
2 c. graham cracker crumbs
1 c. maraschino cherries, chopped
14-oz. can sweetened condensed
    milk

½ c. chopped pecans
3 c. sweetened flaked coconut

Use a mix of red and green cherries for a really festive look.

    In a large bowl, combine marshmallows, cracker crumbs, cherries, condensed milk and pecans; mix well and shape dough into one-inch balls. Place coconut in a shallow dish; roll balls in coconut. Chill 3 hours or until firm. Store in an airtight container in the refrigerator. Makes about 5 dozen.

Michelle Rooney
Sunbury, OH

Cherry Cardamom Cookies

6-oz. jar maraschino cherries,
    drained and diced
2 ⅓ c. plus 2 T. all-purpose
    flour, divided
1 t. baking powder
1 t. cardamom
½ t. baking soda

½ c. butter, softened
1 c. sugar
3-oz. pkg. cream cheese, softened
1 egg
2 T. buttermilk
1 t. almond extract
Garnish: powdered sugar

    In a small bowl, combine cherries and 2 tablespoons flour. Toss to mix; set aside. In a medium bowl, combine remaining flour, baking powder, cardamom and baking soda, stirring to mix. In a large bowl, combine butter, sugar and cream cheese. Beat with an electric mixer at medium speed until fluffy. Add egg, buttermilk and almond extract; beat until blended. Gradually add flour mixture to butter mixture, beating just until moistened; fold in cherry mixture. Chill for one hour. Shape dough into one-inch balls; place on ungreased baking sheets. Bake at 350 degrees for 12 to 14 minutes; remove to wire racks to cool completely. Garnish with powdered sugar. Store in an airtight container. Makes about 3 dozen.

Holly Child
Parker, CO

Snowcap Cookies

These look just like mini mountain peaks! They're a great make-ahead gift because they freeze so well.

¾ c. butter, softened
1 c. sugar
3 eggs
1 t. vanilla extract
6 1-oz. sqs. white baking
    chocolate, melted and cooled

3 ½ c. all-purpose flour
1 t. baking powder
1 t. salt
⅛ t. nutmeg
1 ½ c. chopped walnuts, toasted
Garnish: powdered sugar

In a large bowl, combine butter and sugar. Beat with an electric mixer at medium speed until light and fluffy; add eggs, one at a time, beating until blended after each addition. Stir in vanilla; add melted chocolate, beating 30 seconds. In a separate bowl, combine flour, baking powder, salt and nutmeg, stirring to mix; gradually add flour mixture to butter mixture, beating until blended. Fold in walnuts. Drop by tablespoonfuls onto greased baking sheets. Bake at 350 degrees for 10 to 12 minutes; remove to wire racks to cool completely. Sprinkle tops with powdered sugar. Store in an airtight container. Makes 3 to 4 dozen.

snowcaps in a snow cap!

Wrap a batch of Snowcap Cookies in clear plastic wrap and tuck the package inside a woolly toboggan or stocking cap. Add a package of cocoa mix to help chase away the chills.

a family-style gift

Give the gift of a family movie night! Decorate a new paint pail with paper Christmas cut-outs or painted Christmas designs. Tuck in a classic holiday movie, microwave popcorn and some of your yummiest homemade cookies. Everyone will love it!

Butterscotch Gingerbread Cookies

pictured on page 16

½ c. butter, softened
½ c. brown sugar, packed
3.5-oz. pkg. cook & serve
    butterscotch pudding mix
1 egg, beaten

1 ½ c. all-purpose flour
1 ½ t. ground ginger
1 t. cinnamon
½ t. baking soda

In a large bowl, combine butter, brown sugar and pudding mix. Beat with an electric mixer at medium speed until light and fluffy; add egg and beat well. In a separate bowl, combine flour, ginger, cinnamon and baking soda, stirring to mix. Gradually stir flour mixture into butter mixture, mixing until blended. Chill 30 minutes. Roll dough in batches to ¼-inch thickness on a floured surface; cut with cookie cutters as desired. Place on a greased baking sheet and bake at 350 degrees for 8 to 10 minutes, until golden. Remove to a wire rack to cool completely. Store in an airtight container. Makes about one dozen.

Amy Butcher
Columbus, GA

Ginger-Molasses Cookies

Delicious gingerbread flavor without the work!

¾ c. butter, softened
1 c. brown sugar, packed
1 egg
⅓ c. molasses
2 ½ c. all-purpose flour

2 t. ground ginger
2 t. baking soda
1 t. cinnamon
½ t. salt
½ c. sugar

In a large bowl, beat butter and brown sugar with an electric mixer at medium speed until light and fluffy; add egg and molasses, beating until blended. In a separate bowl, combine flour and next 4 ingredients, stirring to mix. Gradually add flour mixture to butter mixture, stirring just until blended. Chill dough one hour or until firm. Place sugar in a shallow dish. Shape chilled dough into one-inch balls, roll in sugar and place on ungreased baking sheets. Bake at 350 degrees for 15 minutes, or until golden. Cool 2 minutes on pans; remove to wire racks to cool completely. Store in an airtight container. Makes 6 dozen.

Lisa Sett
Thousand Oaks, CA

Nellie's Persimmon Cookies

A ripe persimmon should be soft to the touch and yield between ½ to ¾ cup of pulp.

1 persimmon
1 c. butter, softened
1 c. brown sugar, packed
1 c. sugar

2 eggs, beaten
2 ½ c. all-purpose flour
½ t. baking soda
1 c. chopped pecans

Rinse persimmon under cold water; pat dry. Using a small sharp knife, make an x-shaped cut in the pointed end. Pull back sections of the peel from cut end; discard seeds, peel and stem end. Process pulp in food processor or blender until smooth. Reserve ½ cup persimmon pulp purée; save any remaining pulp purée for another use, if desired. Combine butter and sugars in a large bowl and beat with an electric mixer at medium speed until light and fluffy. Beat in eggs and puréed persimmon pulp. In a separate bowl, combine flour and baking soda, stirring to mix; gradually add flour mixture to butter mixture, beating until blended. Fold in pecans; cover and chill one hour. Drop by teaspoonfuls onto ungreased baking sheets. Press each cookie with a fork dipped in warm water. Bake at 350 degrees for 10 minutes, or until golden. Remove to wire racks to cool. Store in an airtight container. Makes 6 dozen.

Dorothy Ames
Lerna, IL

Nellie's Persimmon Cookies

layers of goodies

A two or three-tier pie stand is ideal for serving a variety of cookies and candies. Set a plate on each tier and fill with goodies galore.

Cool Mint Chocolate Swirls

¾ c. butter
1 ½ c. brown sugar, packed
2 T. water
12-oz. pkg. semi-sweet chocolate
    chips
2 eggs

2 ½ c. all-purpose flour
1 ¼ t. baking soda
½ t. salt
2 4.67-oz. pkgs. crème de menthe
    thins

Cool, refreshing mint wafers top these chocolatey cookies.

In a large saucepan, combine butter, brown sugar and water; place over medium heat and cook, stirring occasionally, until butter melts and mixture is smooth. Remove from heat. Add chocolate chips, stirring until melted; cool 10 minutes. Pour chocolate mixture into a large bowl; add eggs, one at a time, beating by hand until well blended. In a separate bowl, combine flour, baking soda and salt, stirring to mix; add flour mixture to chocolate mixture, stirring well. Cover and chill one hour. Shape dough into walnut-size balls; place 2 inches apart on greased baking sheets. Bake at 350 degrees for 8 to 10 minutes, being careful not to overbake. Press one thin onto each warm cookie and let stand one minute; use the back of a spoon to swirl the softened thin over each cookie. Remove to wire racks to cool completely. Store in an airtight container. Makes 3 dozen.

Regina Vining
Warwick, RI

Powdered Sugar Sandies

Powdered Sugar Sandies

1 c. butter, softened
1 ½ c. powdered sugar, divided
1 t. vanilla extract
2 ¼ c. all-purpose flour
¼ t. salt
Optional: ¾ c. chopped walnuts

In a large bowl, combine butter, ½ cup powdered sugar and vanilla. Beat with an electric mixer at medium speed until creamy. Gradually add flour, salt and nuts, if desired; mix well. Shape dough into one-inch balls and place on ungreased baking sheets. Bake at 400 degrees for 10 to 12 minutes. Place remaining powdered sugar in a bowl. Roll warm cookies in powdered sugar; let cool completely and roll again. Store in an airtight container. Makes 2 to 3 dozen.

Holly Child
Parker, CO

My mom makes these cookies at Christmas-time every year. My first year away at college, I lived in a dorm with a kitchen. I baked these cookies and delivered them to my friends around campus before I headed home for the holidays.
—Holly

Key Lime Bites

¾ c. butter, softened
1 c. powdered sugar, divided
zest of 2 limes
2 T. lime juice
1 T. vanilla extract
1 ¾ c. plus 2 T. all-purpose flour
2 T. cornstarch
½ t. salt

The taste of refreshing key lime pie in a cookie!

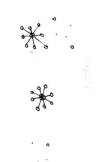

In a large bowl, combine butter and ⅓ cup powdered sugar. Beat with an electric mixer at medium speed until fluffy. Add zest, lime juice and vanilla; beat until blended. In a separate bowl, combine flour, cornstarch and salt, whisking to mix; add flour mixture to butter mixture, stirring until combined. Shape dough into a log and chill one hour. Cut log into ⅛-inch-thick slices; place on parchment-lined baking sheets. Bake at 350 degrees for 12 to 14 minutes, until golden. Remove to wire racks and cool one minute. Place remaining powdered sugar in a large plastic bag; add warm cookies and toss gently to coat. Return to wire racks to cool completely. Store in an airtight container. Makes 2 dozen.

give the taste of summer

Wrap rolls of Key Lime Bites dough in aluminum foil, cover with a layer of fun fabric and tie it all up with a fancy ribbon. Attach the baking instructions and give to a friend who has a sweet tooth!

Buttery Ricotta Cookies

This easy recipe makes very light, soft cookies. So yummy!

½ c. butter, softened
¼ c. ricotta cheese
1 c. sugar
1 egg, beaten

1 t. vanilla extract
2 c. all-purpose flour
½ t. baking soda
½ t. salt

In a large bowl, combine butter and ricotta cheese. Beat with an electric mixer at medium speed until creamy. Gradually add sugar, beating until blended; stir in egg and vanilla. Add remaining ingredients, stirring to blend. Shape dough into one-inch balls and flatten slightly on greased baking sheets. Bake at 350 degrees for 10 minutes, or until edges are golden. Remove to wire racks to cool. Store in an airtight container. Makes about 2 dozen.

April Hale
Kirkwood, NY

Homemade Graham Crackers

Serve with a small bowl of homemade frosting for dipping!

½ c. butter
¾ c. brown sugar, packed
1 t. vanilla extract
2 c. whole-wheat flour
1 c. all-purpose flour

1 t. baking powder
½ t. baking soda
⅛ t. salt
¾ c. milk
Garnish: cinnamon

Combine butter and brown sugar in a large bowl. Beat with an electric mixer at medium speed until fluffy; add vanilla and beat until blended. In a separate bowl, combine flours, baking powder, baking soda and salt, stirring to mix. Gradually add flour mixture to butter mixture alternately with milk, beginning and ending with flour mixture, beating after each addition. Cover dough and chill one hour or until firm. On a lightly floured surface, roll dough to ⅛-inch thickness; cut into 2-inch rectangles and sprinkle with cinnamon. Place crackers ½ inch apart on greased baking sheets. Bake at 350 degrees for 10 to 12 minutes, until edges are golden. Remove to wire racks to cool. Store in an airtight container. Makes 4 dozen.

s'mores on the go

For a yummy gift, pack Homemade Graham Crackers, chocolate candy bars and a jar of marshmallow creme in a handy holiday tote.

to: Beth
from: Missy

Homemade Graham Crackers

Christmas Peppermint & Chocolate Meringues

pictured on page 16

Use the ice pulse button on your blender to make quick work of crushing the candies.

2 egg whites
⅛ t. cream of tartar
⅛ t. salt
¾ c. sugar

½ t. vanilla extract
3 T. crushed peppermint candies
2 c. mini semi-sweet chocolate
    chips

   In a large bowl, beat egg whites with an electric mixer at high speed until foamy. Add cream of tartar and salt, beating until mixed; gradually add sugar, one tablespoon at a time, beating well after each addition until stiff peaks form. Gently fold in remaining ingredients. Drop by teaspoonfuls 1½ inches apart on baking sheets sprayed with non-stick vegetable spray. Bake at 250 degrees for 40 minutes, or until dry. Remove to wire racks to cool completely. Store in an airtight container. Makes 3 dozen.

Peggy Cummings
Cibolo, TX

from cookies to snowmen

Turn meringue cookies into cute snowman faces simply by adding eyes, noses and mouths with mini chocolate chips and red cinnamon candies "glued on" with a bit of frosting.

Chocolate Crunch Brownies,
page 45

Yummy Brownies & Bars

The ultimate chocolate lover's treat; add chewy bars filled with oats, nuts or fruit for some delicious goodness.

Red Velvet Brownies

4-oz. bittersweet chocolate baking bar, chopped	1-oz. bottle red liquid food coloring
¾ c. butter	1 ½ t. baking powder
2 c. sugar	1 t. vanilla extract
4 eggs	⅛ t. salt
1 ½ c. all-purpose flour	Optional: chopped pecans

Line bottom and sides of a 9½"x9½" baking pan with aluminum foil, allowing 2 to 4 inches to extend over sides; lightly grease foil. Microwave chocolate and butter in a large microwave-safe bowl on high 1 ½ to 2 minutes, until melted and smooth, stirring at 30-second intervals. Add sugar, whisking to blend. Add eggs, one at a time, whisking after each addition just until blended. Gently stir in flour and remaining ingredients except pecans. Pour mixture into pan. Bake at 350 degrees for 44 to 48 minutes, until a toothpick inserted in center comes out with a few moist crumbs. Cool completely in pan on a wire rack. Spread with Cream Cheese Frosting; cut into bars. Top with chopped pecans, if desired. Store in refrigerator in an airtight container. Makes 16 servings.

Cream Cheese Frosting

8-oz. pkg. cream cheese, softened	1 ½ c. powdered sugar
3 T. butter, softened	⅛ t. salt
	1 t. vanilla extract

In a large bowl, beat cream cheese and butter with an electric mixer at medium speed until creamy. Gradually add powdered sugar and salt, beating until blended. Stir in vanilla.

Barbara Girlardo
Pittsburgh, PA

festive farewell party treats

Dress up a dessert tray in no time. Place homemade treats in shiny gold or silver paper muffin liners next to the front door for guests to pick up on their way home.

Fudgy Cream Cheese Brownies

⅔ c. butter
4 to 5 T. baking cocoa
6 eggs, divided
2 t. vanilla extract, divided
1¼ c. plus 2 T. all-purpose
    flour, divided

1 t. baking powder
½ t. salt
¾ c. chopped walnuts
8-oz. pkg. cream cheese, softened
½ c. sugar

In a large saucepan, combine butter and cocoa; heat over medium heat until butter melts, stirring often. Remove from heat and cool 5 minutes. Add 4 eggs, one at a time, beating well after each addition. Stir in 1 teaspoon vanilla. In a bowl, combine 1¼ cups flour, baking powder and salt. Gradually add flour mixture to cocoa mixture; fold in nuts. Spread batter into a greased 13"x9" baking pan; set aside.

In a separate bowl, combine cream cheese and sugar; beat with an electric mixer at medium speed until creamy. Add remaining eggs, 2 tablespoons flour and 1 teaspoon vanilla; mix until blended. Spread cream cheese mixture evenly over cocoa mixture in pan; swirl with a knife. Bake at 350 degrees for 35 to 40 minutes, until a toothpick inserted in center tests clean and edges pull away from sides of pan. Cool completely in pan on a wire rack; cut into bars. Store in an airtight container in the refrigerator. Makes one dozen.

Wendy Ross
Boulder Junction, WI

Double-Dark Chocolate Brownies

My grandson just loves these...they are the only dessert he asks for! They are so moist that they don't need any frosting.
—Terri

1½ c. butter, melted
3 c. sugar
2 t. chocolate or vanilla extract
1 t. almond extract
6 eggs, beaten

1½ c. all-purpose flour
1 c. baking cocoa
1½ t. baking powder
1 t. salt
1 c. semi-sweet chocolate chips

In a large bowl, combine melted butter, sugar and extracts; stir well. Add eggs and beat well with a spoon. In a separate bowl, combine flour, cocoa, baking powder and salt. Gradually add flour mixture to butter mixture, beating until well blended. Add chocolate chips and stir well. Spread batter evenly in a greased 13"x9" glass casserole dish. Bake at 350 degrees for 30 to 40 minutes, until a toothpick inserted in center tests clean. Cool completely in pan on a wire rack; cut into bars. Store in an airtight container. Makes 1½ dozen.

Terri Lotz-Ganley
South Euclid, OH

Chocolate Crunch Brownies

pictured on page 40

1 c. butter, softened
2 c. sugar
4 eggs
2 t. vanilla extract
1 c. all-purpose flour
6 T. baking cocoa

½ t. salt
7-oz. jar marshmallow creme
1 c. creamy peanut butter
2 c. semi-sweet chocolate chips
3 c. crispy rice cereal

Chocolate, peanut butter and marshmallow creme...all the essentials of a sweet-tasting treat!

In a large bowl, combine butter and sugar; beat with an electric mixer at medium speed until creamy. Add eggs, one at a time, beating until blended after each addition. Add vanilla. In a separate bowl, combine flour, cocoa and salt; whisk to mix. Gradually add flour mixture to butter mixture. Spread batter into a lightly greased 13"x9" baking pan. Bake at 350 degrees for 35 to 40 minutes, until a toothpick inserted in center comes out with a few moist crumbs. Cool completely in pan on a wire rack. Spread marshmallow creme over brownies. Combine peanut butter and chocolate chips in a saucepan; heat over low heat, stirring constantly, until melted and smooth. Remove from heat; stir in cereal. Spread peanut butter mixture over marshmallow layer and chill until firm. Cut into bars and store in an airtight container in the refrigerator. Makes about 2 ½ dozen.

Lisa Willard
Dunwoody, GA

create handmade gift tags

You'll find all kinds of paper tags, stickers, glitter and trims in the scrapbooking aisle of craft stores...let your imagination go!

Peppermint Bark Brownies

20-oz. pkg. fudge brownie mix
12-oz. pkg. white chocolate chips

2 t. butter
1 ½ c. candy canes, crushed

 Prepare and bake brownie mix in a lightly greased 13"x9" baking pan according to package directions. Cool completely in pan on a wire rack. Combine chocolate chips and butter in a saucepan; heat over low heat until melted, stirring constantly with a rubber spatula. Spread chocolate mixture over brownies; sprinkle with crushed candy. Let stand 30 minutes, or until frosting hardens. Cut into squares; store in an airtight container. Makes 2 dozen.

Angie Biggin
Lyons, IL

Blondies

6 T. butter, melted and cooled
1 egg, beaten
1 c. brown sugar, packed
1 T. hot water
1 t. vanilla extract

1 c. all-purpose flour
½ t. baking powder
¼ T. baking soda
½ t. salt
⅓ c. chocolate chips

 In a large bowl, combine butter, egg, brown sugar, water and vanilla; mix well. Sift together flour, baking powder, baking soda and salt; gradually add flour mixture to sugar mixture, blending well. Pour batter into a greased 8"x8" baking pan; sprinkle with chocolate chips. Bake at 350 degrees for 25 to 30 minutes, until a toothpick inserted in center comes out clean. Cool in pan on a wire rack; cut into bars. Makes one dozen.

Leslie Stimel
Powell, OH

round is nice!

Need a clever way to give a gift of brownies? Cut the brownies with a round cookie cutter. Stack them inside a wide-mouth glass jar, layered with circles of parchment paper or colorful tissue paper.

Brown Sugar Brownies

Brown Sugar Brownies

⅔ c. butter, softened
2 ¼ c. brown sugar, packed
4 eggs
1 t. vanilla extract
2 c. all-purpose flour

2 t. baking powder
1 t. salt
12-oz. pkg. semi-sweet chocolate
  chips

In a large bowl, combine butter and brown sugar; beat with an electric mixer at medium speed until light and fluffy. Beat in eggs, one at a time, just until blended. Beat in vanilla. In a separate bowl, combine flour, baking powder and salt; gradually add flour mixture to butter mixture, stirring until blended. Stir in chocolate chips; spoon batter into a greased 13"x9" baking pan. Bake at 350 degrees for 35 to 40 minutes, until a toothpick inserted in center comes out with a few moist crumbs. Cool completely in pan on a wire rack. Cut into squares. Store in an airtight container. Makes 1 ½ dozen.

Diana Pindell
Wooster, OH

Corny Crunch Bars

If you like sweet & salty treats, you'll love these bars!

2 c. light corn syrup
2 c. sugar
2 c. crunchy peanut butter
2 10.5-oz. pkgs. corn chips

In a large saucepan, combine corn syrup and sugar; bring to a boil over medium heat, stirring occasionally. Remove from heat; stir in peanut butter. Place corn chips in a large bowl coated with non-stick vegetable spray; stir in peanut butter mixture. Gently press into a buttered 18"x12" baking pan. Cool in pan on a wire rack until firm. Cut into squares. Makes 2 dozen.

Jeannine Mertz
Hurdsfield, ND

Apple-Cheddar Bars

Take a basket of these cookies to the bus stop to share with kids on the first day of school.

1 c. brown sugar, packed
2 eggs
3 c. apples, peeled, cored and chopped
1 c. all-purpose flour
2 t. baking powder
1 t. salt
1 c. shredded Cheddar cheese
¾ c. chopped nuts
¼ c. flaked coconut

In a large bowl, combine sugar and eggs; stir well. Fold in apples. In a separate bowl, combine flour, baking powder and salt, stirring to mix. Add cheese, nuts and coconut to flour mixture, stirring to mix. Gradually add flour mixture to apple mixture, stirring just until combined. Spread batter in a greased and floured 13"x9" baking pan. Bake at 375 degrees for 20 to 25 minutes, until a toothpick inserted in center comes out clean. Let cool in pan on a wire rack for 10 minutes; cut into bars. Makes 2 to 3 dozen.

Marie Stewart
Pensacola, FL

easy placecards

Bend a 12-inch green pipe cleaner into a triangular tree shape, twisting the ends together at the center of the base to form the trunk. Insert the trunk into a cork and pin on a namecard with a bulletin board tack. So simple and fun for kids to do!

Corny Crunch Bars

German Apple Streusel Kuchen

German Apple Streusel Kuchen

16-oz. loaf frozen bread
   dough, thawed
4 Granny Smith apples, cored,
   peeled and thinly sliced
¾ c. plus ⅓ c. sugar, divided

1 t. cinnamon
1 T. vanilla extract
¼ c. sliced almonds
1 ¼ c. all-purpose flour
¼ c. butter, melted

Let dough rise according to package directions. Spread dough in a greased 16"x11" baking sheet. Cover dough with plastic wrap and let rise in a warm place (85 degrees), free from drafts, 20 to 25 minutes, until double in bulk. Mix apples, ¾ cup sugar, cinnamon and vanilla; spread apple mixture evenly over dough. Sprinkle with almonds. In a separate bowl, combine flour, butter and remaining sugar; mix until crumbly and spread evenly over apple layer. Bake at 375 degrees for 25 minutes, or until a toothpick inserted in center comes out clean. Cool completely in pan on a wire rack; cut into squares. Makes 2 dozen.

Karin Anderson
Hillsboro, OH

I was born and raised in Germany, so naturally I am always looking for recipes that remind me of my childhood. Baking this cake brings back so many beautiful memories of my parents and brothers.

—Karin

Grandma Gray's Spice-Nut Bars

1 ½ c. all-purpose flour
½ t. baking powder
½ t. baking soda
½ t. salt
½ t. cinnamon
¼ t. nutmeg
⅛ t. ground cloves

¼ c. butter, softened
1 c. brown sugar, packed
1 egg, beaten
½ c. plus 1 T. hot coffee, divided
½ c. raisins
½ c. chopped walnuts
½ c. powdered sugar

In a large bowl, combine flour and baking powder, baking soda, salt, cinnamon, nutmeg and cloves, stirring to mix. In a separate large bowl, beat butter, brown sugar and egg with an electric mixer at medium speed until blended. Add ½ cup coffee and beat well; stir in raisins and walnuts. Gradually add flour mixture to butter mixture. Pour into a greased 13"x9" baking pan. Bake at 350 degrees for 20 to 25 minutes, until golden. In a small bowl, combine powdered sugar and remaining coffee; stir well. Immediately spread glaze over warm bars. Cool in pan on a wire rack and cut into bars. Makes 2 dozen.

Kelly Wood
Salem, OH

This recipe belonged to my great-grandmother on my mother's side. Mother made these cookie bars every Christmas...we always gobbled them up immediately! The aromatic spices of cinnamon, nutmeg and cloves remind me of the holidays.

—Kelly

Applesauce Spice Bars

⅔ c. brown sugar, packed
1 c. all purpose flour
1 t. baking soda
½ t. salt
1 t. pumpkin pie spice

1 c. applesauce
¼ c. butter, softened
1 egg
Optional: 1 c. raisins

In a large bowl, combine all ingredients and raisins if desired; mix thoroughly. Spread batter in a lightly greased 13"x9" baking pan. Bake at 350 degrees for 25 minutes, or until a toothpick inserted in center comes out clean. Cool completely in pan on a wire rack; frost with Browned Butter Frosting. Cut into 3"x1" bars. Makes 2 ½ to 3 dozen.

Browned Butter Frosting

3 T. butter
1 ½ c. powdered sugar

1 t. vanilla extract
1 to 1 ½ T. milk

Melt butter in a medium saucepan over medium heat until light brown in color; remove from heat. Blend in remaining ingredients; beat with an electric mixer at medium speed until frosting is smooth and spreading consistency.

Barbara Wise
Jamestown, OH

I found this recipe more than 35 years ago on the back of a flour bag. These are the bars that my family insists I make whenever we have a family get-together.

—Barbara

honor our service men & women

Wrap up some home-baked treats to send to service persons overseas and tuck in a note that says, "We're thinking of you." They're sure to appreciate your thoughtfulness. The American Red Cross can provide information on how to mail care packages.

Choco-Berry Goodie Bars

3 c. quick-cooking oats, uncooked
14-oz. can sweetened condensed
   milk
2 T. butter, melted
1 c. sweetened flaked coconut

1 c. sliced almonds
1 c. mini semi-sweet chocolate
   chips
½ c. sweetened dried cranberries

In a large bowl, combine all ingredients and use hands to mix well. Press into a greased 13"x9" baking pan. Bake at 350 degrees for 20 to 25 minutes, until edges are golden. Cool 5 minutes; slice into squares and cool completely. Store in an airtight container. Makes 2 dozen.

Brenda Smith
Delaware, OH

It's so easy to change these yummy bars to suit your family's taste... try using chopped walnuts or pecans instead of almonds and chopped dried apricots or pineapple instead of cranberries.

Teresa's Tasty Apricot Bars

½ c. butter, softened
1 c. all-purpose flour
1 t. baking powder

1 egg, beaten
1 T. milk
¾ c. apricot preserves

In a large bowl, combine butter, flour and baking powder; beat with an electric mixer at medium speed until blended. Stir in egg and milk. Press into a lightly greased 9"x9" baking pan; spread preserves over top and set aside. Prepare Coconut Topping and spread over preserves. Bake at 350 degrees for 25 to 30 minutes, until a toothpick inserted in center comes out clean. Cool completely in pan on a wire rack. Cut into bars. Makes one dozen.

Coconut Topping

¼ c. butter, softened
1 c. sugar
1 egg, beaten

1 t. vanilla extract
1 c. sweetened flaked coconut

In a bowl, combine butter and sugar, stirring until blended. Add egg and vanilla; stir well. Add coconut and stir until well blended.

Teresa Stiegelmeyer
Indianapolis, IN

Sweet Raspberry-Oat Bars

½ c. butter
1 c. brown sugar, packed
1 ½ c. all-purpose flour
½ t. baking soda
½ t. salt

1 ½ c. long-cooking oats,
  uncooked
¼ c. water
⅔ c. seedless raspberry jam
1 t. lemon juice

In a large bowl, combine butter and brown sugar; beat with an electric mixer at medium speed until light and fluffy. In a separate bowl, combine flour, baking soda and salt; stir to mix. Add flour mixture into butter mixture, stirring to blend. Add oats and water; mix until crumbly. Firmly pat half of oat mixture into the bottom of a greased 13"x9" baking pan. In a small bowl, combine jam and lemon juice; stir to blend. Spread jam mixture over oat mixture. Sprinkle remaining oat mixture over top. Bake at 350 degrees for 25 minutes, or until a toothpick inserted in center comes out clean. Cool completely in pan on a wire rack; cut into bars. Makes 2 ½ dozen.

Kathleen Sturm
Corona, CA

Rocky Road Crunch Bars

Stir in some red and green chocolate-coated candies for a holiday touch.

⅓ c. honey
3 T. butter
4 c. mini marshmallows
4 c. granola or oat cluster cereal

2 T. creamy or crunchy peanut
  butter
4 1-oz. sqs. semi-sweet baking
  chocolate, chopped

In a microwave-safe bowl, combine honey and butter; microwave on high one minute; stir until well blended. Add marshmallows; toss gently to coat. Microwave on high 90 seconds, or until marshmallows puff. Stir in remaining ingredients. Press into a greased 13"x9" baking pan; chill until firm. Cut into bars. Makes 2 dozen.

Angie Biggin
Lyons, IL

Sweet Raspberry-Oat
Bars

Coconut-Pecan Fudge Bars

15.25-oz. pkg. chocolate fudge
  cake mix
15-oz. container coconut-pecan
  frosting

1 c. applesauce
1 egg, beaten
Optional: powdered sugar

In a large bowl, combine all ingredients and mix well; spread in a lightly greased 13"x9" baking pan. Bake at 350 degrees for 30 to 32 minutes, until a toothpick inserted in center comes out clean. Cool for one hour; cut into 2-inch squares. Top with powdered sugar, if desired. Makes 2 dozen.

Linda Nichols
Wintersville, OH

Chocolate-Mint Candy Brownies

1 ½ c. butter, melted
3 c. sugar
2 t. vanilla extract
5 eggs, beaten
1 c. all-purpose flour
1 c. baking cocoa

1 t. baking powder
1 t. salt
24 chocolate-covered mint patties,
    unwrapped
Optional: chocolate-covered mint
    patties, chopped

In a large bowl, combine butter, sugar and vanilla; stir to mix. Add eggs and blend well. Combine flour, cocoa, baking powder and salt in a separate bowl. Gradually add flour mixture to butter mixture; stir until blended. Reserve 2 cups of batter; spread remaining batter in a greased 13"x9" baking pan. Place chocolate-covered mint patties over batter in a single layer; spread reserved batter over patties. Bake at 350 degrees for 50 to 55 minutes, until brownies begin to pull away from sides of pan. Cool completely in pan on a wire rack before cutting. Garnish with chopped chocolate-covered mint patties, if desired. Store in an airtight container. Makes 3 dozen.

Summer Staib
Broomfield, CO

Fruity Popcorn Bars

3-oz. pkg. microwave popcorn, popped
¾ c. white chocolate chips
¾ c. sweetened dried cranberries
½ c. sweetened flaked coconut
½ c. slivered almonds, coarsely chopped
10-oz. pkg. marshmallows
3 T. butter

Line bottom and sides of a 13"x9" baking pan with aluminum foil, allowing 2 to 4 inches to extend over the edges; spray lightly with non-stick vegetable cooking spray. In a large bowl, combine all ingredients except marshmallows and butter; toss to mix. In a large saucepan, combine marshmallows and butter; heat over medium heat, stirring until smooth. Pour marshmallow mixture over popcorn mixture and toss to coat completely; quickly pour into prepared pan. Press a sheet of wax paper firmly on top of popcorn mixture. Chill for 30 minutes, or until firm. Using foil as handles, lift chilled mixture from pan; peel off foil and wax paper. Slice into bars and chill an additional 30 minutes. Makes 16.

Melody Taynor
Everett, WA

share a bag

Spoon the dry ingredients for Fruity Popcorn Bars into separate plastic zipping bags and nestle them in a cheery red mixing bowl along with the packages of marshmallows and unpopped popcorn. Tie on a recipe card for a gift anyone is sure to love!

Pecan Turtles, page 66
Grandma's Peanut Brittle, page 65

Katherine

Old-Fashioned Candies

These sweet goodies, meant to be shared with kids and grown-ups alike, make year-round gift-giving extra special.

Mocha-Pecan Fudge

3 6-oz. pkgs. semi-sweet
   chocolate chips
14-oz. can sweetened condensed
   milk
2 T. strong brewed coffee, cooled

1 t. cinnamon
⅛ t. salt
1 c. toasted chopped pecans
1 t. vanilla extract

In a large microwave-safe bowl, combine chocolate chips, condensed milk, coffee, cinnamon and salt. Microwave chocolate mixture in a large microwave-safe bowl on high 1 ½ minutes until melted and smooth, stirring at 30-second intervals. Stir in pecans and vanilla; immediately spread into a greased aluminum foil-lined 8"x8" baking pan. Cover and chill until firm, about 2 hours. Remove from pan; cut into one-inch squares. Store in an airtight container at room temperature. Makes about 5 dozen.

Double Chocolate-Orange Fudge

A blend of white and semi-sweet chocolate makes this fudge creamy and oh-so rich!

14-oz. can sweetened condensed
   milk, divided
8 1-oz. sqs. semi-sweet baking
   chocolate

½ c. chopped walnuts
1 t. vanilla extract
6 1-oz. sqs. white baking chocolate
2 t. orange zest

Line the bottom and sides of an 8"x8" baking pan with aluminum foil, allowing 2 to 4 inches to extend over edges of pan; spray lightly with non-stick vegetable cooking spray. Pour ¾ cup milk into a 4-cup glass measuring cup; add semi-sweet chocolate and microwave on high 3 minutes, or until chocolate melts and mixture is smooth, stirring every minute. Add walnuts and vanilla, stirring to mix; pour mixture into prepared pan. Chill until slightly firm. Combine remaining milk and white chocolate in a microwave-safe bowl; microwave on high 1 ½ to 2 minutes, until chocolate is melted and smooth, stirring at 30-second intervals. Stir in zest and spread evenly over chocolate layer. Chill 2 hours or until firm; cut into squares. Store in an airtight container in the refrigerator. Makes 1 ½ dozen.

Karen Whitby
Charlotte, VT

a perfect pairing

Want to bring a little sunshine to friends in the middle of winter? Give them Double Chocolate-Orange Fudge with some clementines in a wooden crate. You'll definitely receive lots of smiles.

Double Chocolate-Orange
Fudge

Add a whimsical touch to a Christmas tree or stack of gifts by using fabric paint to write the words of a favorite Christmas carol on a long length of wide ribbon. Wrap the ribbon around gifts or use as a garland for the tree.

Cookies & Cream Truffles

These have become a staple at our house every holiday.

—Sally

8-oz. pkg. cream cheese, softened
4 c. chocolate sandwich cookies, crushed
2 c. white chocolate chips
1 T. shortening

In a large bowl, beat cream cheese with an electric mixer at medium speed until fluffy; blend in crushed cookies. Chill 2 hours; shape chilled dough into one-inch balls. In the top of a double boiler, combine chocolate chips and shortening; cook over medium heat until chips melt, stirring constantly. Dip balls into chocolate mixture to coat; place on wax paper until chocolate sets. Store in an airtight container in the refrigerator. Makes 2 ½ dozen.

Sally Swift
Jacksonville, FL

Bourbon Balls

Try rolling these balls in baking cocoa or fine, colored sugars instead of powdered sugar.

1 c. powdered sugar
2 T. baking cocoa
2 c. vanilla wafers, crushed
1 c. chopped pecans
¼ c. bourbon or 2 to 4 t. vanilla extract
2 T. light corn syrup
powdered sugar

In a large bowl, sift together one cup powdered sugar and cocoa. Add crushed wafers and pecans; mix well. Add bourbon or vanilla and corn syrup, stirring until well mixed; shape into one-inch balls. Place powdered sugar in a shallow dish; roll the balls in powdered sugar until coated. Place on wax paper until set completely before serving. Store in an airtight container. Makes 3 dozen.

Kim Schooler
Norman, OK

Almond Brittle

1 ½ c. whole almonds
3 T. butter

1 c. sugar
4 T. water

Spread almonds in a single layer on an ungreased baking sheet; bake at 350 degrees for 10 minutes, stirring occasionally. In a large skillet, melt butter over medium heat. Add toasted almonds and cook for 3 minutes, stirring constantly; set aside. In a large, heavy saucepan, combine sugar and water; bring to a boil, stirring to dissolve sugar. Wash down crystals on sides of pan with a small brush dipped in hot water; do not stir. Continue boiling until mixture turns golden. Remove from heat; add the butter-almond mixture, stirring to mix. Quickly pour onto a greased baking sheet. Cool until hardened; break into pieces. Store at room temperature in an airtight container. Makes about one pound.

Susan White
Lexington, KY

Grandma's Peanut Brittle

pictured on page 60

2 c. sugar
1 c. light corn syrup
½ c. water
12-oz. can cocktail peanuts

¼ c. butter, softened
1 ½ t. baking soda
½ t. salt

In a heavy saucepan, combine sugar, corn syrup and water; cook over medium heat until mixture reaches the hard-ball stage, or 250 to 269 degrees on a candy thermometer, stirring constantly. Add peanuts and cook until mixture reaches the hard-crack stage, or 290 to 310 degrees. Remove from heat. Add butter, baking soda and salt, stirring to mix. Pour into an ungreased 15"x10" jelly-roll pan. Cool and break into pieces. Makes 3 dozen.

Janet Haynes
Bowling Green, KY

Everyone looked forward to receiving my grandmother's peanut brittle as part of their Christmas gift. People still ask me for her recipe, even 30 years later!
—Janet

add some jingle cheer!

Slip a plastic zip-top bag of Grandma's Peanut Brittle inside a red paper sack, fold the top over and punch holes across the top at one-inch intervals. Thread a large needle with thin ribbon and weave it through the holes to close, adding jingle bells along the way.

Pecan Turtles

pictured on page 60

14-oz. pkg. caramels, wrappers
    removed
¼ c. evaporated milk
2 c. pecan halves

6-oz. pkg. semi-sweet chocolate
    chips
2 T. shortening

In a medium saucepan, combine caramels and evaporated milk; cook over low heat until caramels melt, stirring frequently. Add nuts, stirring to combine. Remove from heat. Drop by teaspoonfuls onto buttered wax paper; refrigerate until firm. In a separate medium saucepan, combine chocolate chips and shortening; cook over low heat until chocolate chips and shortening melt, stirring until smooth. Dip candies into chocolate mixture and return them to wax paper to set. Store at room temperature in an airtight container. Makes about 2 pounds.

Lisa Lindsey
Limestone, ME

There's nothing slow about these turtles... they disappear quickly!

Creamy Butter Mints

16-oz. pkg. powdered sugar
½ c. butter, softened
2 T. whipping cream

¼ t. peppermint extract
2 drops red food coloring

In a medium bowl, combine powdered sugar and butter; beat with an electric mixer at medium speed for 2 to 3 minutes, until blended and creamy. Add cream, extract and food coloring; beat for 3 to 4 minutes, until well blended. Shape mixture into ½-inch balls; lightly press balls with thumb to form wafers. Place on wire racks and let dry overnight, uncovered. Store in an airtight container. Makes 5 dozen.

Betty Wachowiak
Waukegan, IL

Vary the food coloring depending on the occasion...pastels are just perfect for springtime or a bridal shower.

Cranberry Poppers

16-oz. pkg. cranberries

14-oz. pkg. white melting
    chocolate, melted

Rinse cranberries; pat dry. Dip each cranberry into chocolate and place on wax paper to dry. Store in an airtight container in the refrigerator. Makes about 1 ½ pounds.

Marj Miller
Tyler, TX

Cashew-Macadamia Crunch

Cashew-Macadamia Crunch

12-oz. pkg. milk chocolate chips
½ c. butter, softened
½ c. sugar
2 T. light corn syrup

¾ c. cashews, coarsely chopped
¾ c. macadamia nuts, coarsely
    chopped

   Line bottom and sides of a 9"x9" baking pan with aluminum foil, allowing 2 to 4 inches to extend over edges of pan; spray lightly with non-stick vegetable cooking spray. Sprinkle chocolate chips in pan; set aside. In a skillet, combine butter, sugar, corn syrup and nuts; cook over low heat until butter melts and sugar dissolves, stirring constantly. Increase heat to medium and cook until mixture begins to cling together and turns golden, stirring constantly. Pour butter mixture over chocolate chips in pan, spreading evenly. Cool for 15 minutes. Using foil as handles, lift candy from pan; peel off foil. Break into pieces. Store in an airtight container. Makes about 2 pounds.

Marilyn Miller
Fort Washington, PA

Sparkling Sugarplums

Chestnut Truffles

½ c. whipping cream
8-oz. pkg. semi-sweet baking
    chocolate, chopped
2 T. dark corn syrup

12 chestnuts packed in syrup,
    drained, patted dry and
    coarsely chopped
¼ c. powdered sugar
¼ c. baking cocoa

In a small saucepan, bring whipping cream to a simmer over medium heat. Remove from heat; stir in chocolate and corn syrup, stirring until chocolate melts. Fold in chestnuts and pour into a medium bowl; chill one hour. Scoop mixture by 2 teaspoonfuls and form into one-inch balls; place on parchment-lined baking sheets. Chill 15 to 30 minutes, until firm. In a shallow bowl, combine powdered sugar and cocoa, stirring to mix; roll truffles in powdered sugar mixture, coating completely. Store in an airtight container in refrigerator or a cool, dry place. Makes about 2 dozen.

Sharon Demers
Dolores, CO

You can make this up to five days in advance, but do not roll the truffles in the powdered sugar mixture until ready to serve.

Sparkling Sugarplums

1 c. dried apricots
½ c. pitted dates
½ c. golden raisins
1 c. pecans

2 c. vanilla wafers, crushed
1 c. sweetened flaked coconut
½ c. orange juice
½ c. sugar

Combine apricots, dates, raisins and pecans in a food processor; process until finely chopped and place in a large bowl. Add crushed wafers and stir to mix. Add coconut and orange juice; toss to mix. Shape into ¾-inch balls. Place sugar in a shallow dish; roll balls in sugar and place in paper mini muffin liners. Makes about 4 dozen.

Rogene Rogers
Bemidji, MN

I wrap these candies individually in little squares of plastic wrap and tie them with gold cord. Then I arrange them in a fancy dish next to a note that reads, "While visions of sugarplums danced in their heads..."
—Rogene

neat idea

Just for fun, nestle Sparkling Sugarplums in the compartments of a festive red plastic ice cube tray.

Maple Cream Candy

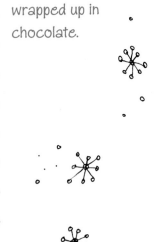

½ c. butter
2 T. maple flavoring
16-oz. pkg. powdered sugar
2 to 3 t. water

12-oz. pkg. semi-sweet chocolate chips
⅓ bar paraffin wax
Optional: pecan halves

In a large bowl, combine butter and flavoring; beat with an electric mixer at medium speed until creamy. Add sugar and beat until well mixed. Add water, one teaspoon at a time, and blend until mixture resembles clay. Pinch off pieces and shape into one-inch balls; flatten and place on a wax paper-lined baking sheet. Chill 30 minutes. In the top of a double boiler, combine chocolate chips and paraffin; cook over medium heat until chocolate and paraffin melt, stirring until blended. Use a toothpick or candy dipper to dip balls into chocolate mixture, coating completely. Top with pecan halves, if desired. Chill until chocolate is set. Store in an airtight container in refrigerator. Makes 5 to 6 dozen.

Cyndi Little
Whitsett, NC

Royal Coconut Creme

Always make candy just one batch at a time. Don't be tempted to double or triple the recipe because the candy may fail to set up properly.

3 c. sugar
6 T. butter, softened
1½ c. whipping cream

⅛ t. salt
1 t. vanilla extract
2 c. sweetened flaked coconut

In a heavy saucepan, combine sugar, butter, cream and salt; bring to a boil over medium-high heat until mixture reaches the soft-ball stage, or 234 to 243 degrees on a candy thermometer, stirring constantly. Remove from heat and let stand 5 minutes. Stir in vanilla and beat by hand or with an electric mixer at medium speed until thick and creamy. Add coconut and stir until well mixed. Pour into a buttered 13"x9" baking pan. Cover and let stand overnight. Cut into bite-size pieces to serve. Store in an airtight container in refrigerator. Makes 2 pounds.

Dorothy McConnell
Brooklyn, IA

Snowstorm Hard Candy

powdered sugar
3 ½ c. sugar
1 c. light corn syrup

1 c. water
1 t. favorite candy flavoring oil
few drops desired food coloring

Grease a heavy 15"x11" jelly-roll pan; dust with powdered sugar and set aside. In a heavy saucepan, combine sugar, corn syrup and water, stirring to mix; cook over medium heat until mixture reaches the hard-crack stage, or 290 to 310 degrees on a candy thermometer, stirring constantly. Remove from heat. Stir in flavoring oil and food coloring until mixture reaches desired shade. Take pan outside and set on the snow on a sidewalk or other flat surface. Using potholders, pour hot candy onto prepared jelly-roll pan; candy will cool quickly. Break into bite-size pieces. Store in an airtight container. Makes 4 cups.

Marcia Bills
Orleans, NE

My three daughters always ask to make this at least once every winter during a snow-storm. It's great fun to make...they love to hear that cracking sound when the hot candy hits the pan! Maple, cinnamon and butter rum are some flavors they especially like.

—Marcia

warm & sweet

Stitch a simple snowflake pattern on a pair of blue mittens with white yarn and tuck packaged Snowstorm Hard Candy inside. The mittens will make a useful gift long after the goodies have been enjoyed!

Puffy Marshmallow Cut-Outs

Mom's Peanut Butter Candy

1 c. creamy peanut butter
1 c. powdered sugar

1 T. half-and-half
24 pecan halves

In a medium bowl, combine peanut butter and powdered sugar, stirring to blend. Add half-and-half and mix with hands until well blended. Shape mixture into a ball and roll into a log one-inch in diameter and 24 inches long. Cut into bite-size pieces; press a pecan half onto each piece. Makes 2 dozen.

Patricia Woolsey
Hanover, MI

Puffy Marshmallow Cut-Outs

¾ c. water
4 envs. unflavored gelatin
3 c. sugar
1 ¼ c. light corn syrup

¼ t. salt
2 t. vanilla extract
1 ½ c. powdered sugar, divided

Spray a 13"x9" baking pan with non-stick vegetable spray. Line bottom and sides of pan with wax paper, allowing 2 to 4 inches to extend over edges of pan; coat wax paper with non-stick vegetable spray and set aside. Pour water into a large bowl and sprinkle gelatin over top; let stand 5 minutes. In a heavy saucepan, combine sugar, corn syrup, salt and vanilla; bring to a boil over high heat and cook until mixture reaches the soft-ball stage, or 234 to 243 degrees on a candy thermometer, stirring occasionally. Pour the hot mixture slowly into the gelatin mixture and beat by hand or with an electric mixer at medium speed for 10 minutes, or until very stiff. Pour into prepared pan; smooth top with a spatula. Let stand, uncovered, overnight or until mixture becomes firm. Invert the baking pan onto a surface coated with one cup powdered sugar; peel off wax paper. Lightly coat the insides of desired cookie cutters with non-stick vegetable spray and cut out marshmallows. Place remaining powdered sugar in a shallow dish; roll marshmallow cut-outs in powdered sugar to coat. Makes about 2 dozen.

Anna Burns
Delaware, OH

Back in the early 1950s, my mother made this candy for the fall festivals. It was always one of the first treats to sell out, and I remember I was always so proud of her.

—Patricia

Coffee Toffee

My husband loves to roast his own coffee beans, and we decided to try adding them to a favorite toffee recipe. The result is delicious!

—Sharon

1 c. espresso beans, slightly crushed
½ c. butter
¾ c. brown sugar, packed
1 c. semi-sweet chocolate chips

Sprinkle crushed coffee beans evenly over the bottom of an ungreased 8"x8" baking pan. In a large saucepan, combine butter and brown sugar; bring to a boil over medium-low heat and cook, for exactly 7 minutes, stirring constantly. Immediately pour mixture over crushed beans and quickly spread from side to side of pan. Sprinkle evenly with chocolate chips. Cover pan and let stand 5 minutes. Remove cover and spread melted chocolate chips evenly over the toffee. Chill at least one or up to 3 hours. Invert pan and break toffee into pieces. Makes about one pound.

Sharon Demers
Dolores, CO

Peppermint Bark

2 12-oz. pkgs. white chocolate
   chips
1 t. peppermint extract
½ c. candy canes, crushed

Microwave chocolate chips in a microwave-safe bowl for 1 ½ to 2 minutes, until melted and smooth, stirring at 30-second intervals. Add extract and crushed candy to melted chocolate, stirring to blend. Pour onto a parchment-lined baking sheet. Chill 2 hours; break into pieces. Store in an airtight container in refrigerator. Makes 10 to 12 servings.

Andrea Gordon
Lewis Center, OH

Christmas Crunch

3 c. doughnut-shaped oat cereal
3 c. bite-size corn cereal squares
3 c. bite-size crispy rice cereal
   squares
2 c. salted peanuts
12-oz. pkg. candy-coated
   chocolates
1 ½ lbs. white melting chocolate
   disks

In a large bowl, combine all ingredients except chocolate disks; stir to mix. Microwave chocolate disks in a microwave-safe bowl on high 2 to 3 minutes, until melted and smooth, stirring at 30-second intervals. Pour melted chocolate over cereal mixture; stir gently to coat. Pour onto wax paper; let stand until hardened. Break into pieces; store in airtight containers. Makes about 16 cups.

Julia Leone
Fairport, NY

Coffee Toffee

Blue-Ribbon Cakes & Pies

These sweet gifts become even sweeter when you embellish them with a beautiful serving plate or personalized tag.

Sunny Lemon Cake, page 85

Christmas Rainbow Cake

18½-oz. pkg. moist white cake
  mix
3-oz. pkg. raspberry gelatin mix
2 c. boiling water, divided

3-oz. pkg. lime gelatin mix
12-oz. container frozen whipped
  topping, thawed

For a festive touch, roll out green and red gumdrops and then cut them to resemble holly leaves and berries.

Prepare cake mix and bake in 2 greased 8" round cake pans, according to package directions. Cool in pans 10 minutes; remove from pans and cool completely on wire racks.

Clean pans and return cake layers, top sides up, to pans; prick each layer with a fork every half-inch. In a small bowl, combine raspberry gelatin mix and one cup boiling water, stirring until gelatin dissolves; pour raspberry gelatin over one layer. In another small bowl, combine lime gelatin mix and remaining one cup boiling water, stirring until gelatin dissolves; pour lime gelatin over second layer. Chill layers 3 to 4 hours.

Dip one cake pan into a pan of warm water to loosen cake; invert onto a plate and remove pan. Spread one cup whipped topping on top of layer. Dip second cake pan into warm water, invert on top of first layer and remove pan. Spread remaining topping on top and sides of cake. Serves 6 to 8.

Karen Whitby
Charlotte, VT

holiday spirit

Serve this festive cake adorned with the colors of the season for the perfect sweet ending from your holiday buffet table.

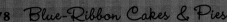

Three-Layer Chocolate Cake

1 c. butter, softened
1 ¾ c. sugar
3 eggs
1 T. vanilla extract
2 ¼ c. all-purpose flour

1 c. baking cocoa
1 ½ t. baking powder
1 t. baking soda
¼ t. salt
1 ¾ c. milk

In a large bowl, beat butter with an electric mixer at medium speed until creamy. Gradually add sugar, beating well after each addition. Add eggs, one at a time, beating until blended after each addition. Add vanilla, beating until blended. In a separate bowl, sift together flour and remaining ingredients except milk. Add flour mixture to butter mixture alternately with milk, beginning and ending with flour mixture, beating until blended after each addition. Pour batter into 3 greased 9" round cake pans.

Bake at 350 degrees for 25 to 30 minutes, until a toothpick inserted in center comes out clean. Cool in pans on a wire rack 10 minutes. Remove from pans and cool on wire racks one hour, or until completely cool. Spread Fudge Frosting on top and sides of cake. Serves 12.

Fudge Frosting

1 c. butter, softened
4 c. powdered sugar, divided
½ c. baking cocoa

4 to 5 T. milk
2 t. vanilla extract

In a large bowl, beat butter with an electric mixer at medium speed until fluffy; gradually add 2 cups powdered sugar and cocoa and beat at medium speed until combined. Gradually add milk and remaining powdered sugar, beating at low speed after each addition until blended. Stir in vanilla.

Pam Vienneau
Derby, CT

sweet handprints

To make the sweetest gift tags, trace the little hands of your kids or grandkids on cardstock.

Italian Cream Cake

2 c. sugar
½ c. butter, softened
½ c. shortening
½ c. buttermilk
2 c. all-purpose flour
1 t. baking soda

½ t. salt
5 eggs, separated
1 c. chopped pecans
2 c. sweetened flaked coconut

In a large bowl, combine sugar, butter, shortening and buttermilk. Beat with an electric mixer at medium speed until blended; set aside. In a separate bowl, combine flour, baking soda and salt, stirring to mix. Gradually add flour mixture and egg yolks to butter mixture, beating until well blended. Stir in pecans and coconut; set aside. In a medium bowl, beat egg whites with clean beaters with an electric mixer at high speed until stiff peaks form. Fold egg whites into batter and pour into 2 greased and floured 8" round cake pans.

Bake at 350 degrees for 40 to 45 minutes, until a toothpick inserted in center comes out clean. Cool in pans on wire racks 10 minutes. Remove from pans and cool on wire racks one hour, or until completely cool. Spread Cream Cheese-Pecan Frosting between layers and on top and sides of cake. Serves 8 to 10.

Cream Cheese-Pecan Frosting

8-oz. pkg. cream cheese, softened
½ c. butter
1 t. vanilla extract

1 lb. powdered sugar
1 c. chopped pecans

In a large bowl, combine cream cheese, butter and vanilla; beat with an electric mixer at medium speed until creamy. Gradually add powdered sugar, beating until fluffy after each addition. Stir in pecans until blended.

Kim Schooler
Norman, OK

Eggnog Pound Cake

Eggnog Pound Cake

Toast slices of this yummy holiday cake for a perfect morning breakfast treat.

1 c. butter, softened
3 c. sugar
6 eggs, beaten
3 c. all-purpose flour
1 c. eggnog

1 t. lemon extract
1 t. vanilla extract
1 t. coconut extract
1 c. sweetened flaked coconut
Optional: powdered sugar

In a large bowl, beat butter with an electric mixer at medium speed until creamy. Gradually add sugar, beating until fluffy after each addition. Add eggs, one at a time, beating just until blended. Add flour to butter mixture alternately with eggnog, beginning and ending with flour, beating at low speed just until blended. Stir in extracts and coconut. Pour into a greased and floured 10" tube pan.

Bake at 325 degrees for 1 ½ hours, or until a toothpick inserted in center comes out clean. Cool in pan on a wire rack 10 minutes; remove from pan and cool completely. Lightly sprinkle with powdered sugar, if desired. Serves 12 to 14.

Nancy Cohrs
Donna, TX

Sunny Lemon Cake

pictured on page 76

1 ½ c. butter, softened
3 c. sugar
5 eggs
3 c. all-purpose flour
¾ c. lemon-lime soda
2 T. lemon extract
1 t. lemon zest
Optional: powdered sugar

In a large bowl, beat butter with an electric mixer at medium speed until creamy. Gradually add sugar, beating until light and fluffy. Add eggs, one at a time, beating well after each addition. Add flour, one cup at a time, beating well after each addition; add lemon-lime soda, lemon extract and lemon zest, beating well. Pour into a greased and floured 10" fluted pan.

Bake at 350 degrees for one hour, or until a toothpick inserted in center comes out clean. Cool in pan on a wire rack 10 minutes; loosen sides of cake. Remove from pan and cool completely. Lightly sprinkle with powdered sugar, if desired. Serves 12.

Leslie Stimel
Gooseberry Patch

Cranberry Swirl Cake

½ c. butter
1 c. sugar
2 eggs
1 t. almond extract
2 c. flour
1 t. baking powder
1 t. baking soda
½ t. salt
1 c. sour cream
8-oz. can whole-berry cranberry
  sauce
½ c. chopped pecans

> So refreshingly different from other cakes, this recipe has always been a must-have for me.
>
> —Mariah

In a large bowl, combine butter and sugar. Beat with an electric mixer at medium speed until light and fluffy. Add eggs, one at a time, beating well after each addition. Add extract and beat well. In a separate bowl, combine flour, baking powder, baking soda and salt, stirring to mix; add flour mixture to butter mixture alternately with sour cream, beginning and ending with flour mixture, beating well after each addition. Spoon half of batter into a greased and floured 10" tube pan; spread cranberry sauce over top and add remaining batter. Sprinkle with pecans.

Bake at 350 degrees for 50 to 55 minutes. Cool in pan on a wire rack 10 minutes; remove from pan and cool on a wire rack one hour, or until completely cool. Serves 8 to 10.

Mariah Thompson
Smyrna, GA

Orange Puff Cupcakes

⅓ c. butter or margarine, softened
1 c. sugar
2 eggs, beaten
1 ¾ c. all-purpose flour
1 t. baking soda

1 T. baking powder
½ c. frozen orange juice
   concentrate, thawed
Vanilla Buttercream Frosting
Garnish: assorted sprinkles

This drool-worthy cupcake is a heavenly citrus delight that will not disappoint even the most avid citrus lovers.

    Beat together margarine and sugar in a bowl; add eggs. Combine flour and baking powder; add alternately with orange juice to margarine mixture. Fill paper-lined muffin cups ⅔ full.
    Bake at 375 degrees for 15 minutes. Let cool. Spread with frosting and garnish with assorted sprinkles, if desired. Makes one dozen.

Vanilla Buttercream Frosting

1 c. butter, softened
2 16-oz. packages powdered
   sugar

2 to 3 T. milk
1 T. vanilla extract
Optional: yellow food coloring

    Beat butter at medium speed with an electric mixer until creamy; gradually add powdered sugar alternately with milk, beating at low speed until blended after each addition. Stir in vanilla extract. Add 2 to 3 drops of food coloring, if desired. Makes about 6 cups.

Heather Roberts
Quebec, Canada

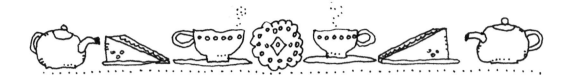

Double-Chocolate Mousse Cake

16-oz. pkg. semi-sweet chocolate
    chips
2 c. butter
1 c. half-and-half
1 c. sugar

1 T. vanilla extract
½ t. salt
8 eggs, beaten
Garnish: whipped topping and
    strawberries

    In a heavy saucepan, combine all ingredients except eggs and garnish.
Cook over low heat until chocolate chips melt, stirring frequently. Cool to
room temperature; fold in eggs. Butter a 9"x3" springform pan; line bottom
with parchment paper. Pour chocolate mixture into prepared pan; bake at
350 degrees for 45 minutes, or until firm. Cool to room temperature. Spread
Chocolate Topping on top of cooled cake. Chill, covered, 4 hours, or until
firm; carefully remove pan. Cut into slices and garnish with whipped topping and strawberries before serving. Serves 10.

Chocolate Topping

1 c. chocolate chips
2 T. butter

2 T. corn syrup
3 T. half-and-half

    In the top of a double boiler, combine chocolate chips, butter and corn
syrup; cook over medium heat until chocolate and butter melt, stirring to
blend. Remove from heat. Add half-and-half, stirring until smooth.

Jessica Jones
York, PA

a welcome gift

You'll receive high praise when you bring this indulgent
chocolate treat to a new neighbor. Be sure to attach
the recipe...this one's a keeper.

Sweet Potato Pie

Chocolate Spice Cake

18 ¼-oz. German chocolate
    cake mix
1 ½ t. cinnamon

3 eggs, lightly beaten
21-oz. can raisin pie filling

A delicious Bundt® cake...dust it with powdered sugar and give it the place of honor on your holiday dessert table.

    In a large bowl, combine cake mix and cinnamon; mix well. Add eggs and pie filling, stirring just until dry ingredients are moistened. Pour mixture into a greased 10" tube pan or 10-cup Bundt® pan. Bake at 350 degrees for 55 minutes to one hour, until a toothpick inserted in center comes out clean. Cool completely in pan on a wire rack. Serves 8 to 10.

Judy Kelly
Saint Charles, MO

Sweet Potato Pie

¼ c. butter, softened
⅓ c. honey
⅛ t. salt
2 c. sweet potatoes, cooked and
    mashed
3 eggs, beaten
½ c. milk

1 t. vanilla extract
½ t. cinnamon
½ t. nutmeg
½ t. ground ginger
9-inch pie crust
Optional: 1 c. pecan halves

    In a large bowl, combine butter, honey and salt; beat with an electric mixer at medium speed until creamy. In a separate bowl, combine sweet potatoes, eggs, milk, vanilla, cinnamon, nutmeg and ginger, stirring well; add sweet potato mixture to butter mixture, stirring well. Pour into unbaked pie crust; sprinkle with pecan halves, if desired. Bake at 375 degrees for 50 to 55 minutes, until center is set. Cool completely on a wire rack. Store in refrigerator. Serves 8.

Barb Kietzer
Niles, MI

shiny crust

Make a fruit pie even more irresistible by brushing peach or apricot syrup on top while the crust is warm and then sprinkling lightly with sugar.

Maple-Pecan Pie

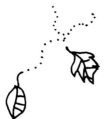

This pie tastes great anytime, but it seems to be just about perfect when served warm on a chilly day.

4 eggs
⅔ c. sugar
6 T. butter, melted
1 c. maple syrup
½ t. salt
1 ½ c. pecan halves
9-inch pie crust
Garnish: whipped topping

In a large bowl, combine eggs, sugar, melted butter, maple syrup and salt; whisk until thoroughly blended. Sprinkle pecan halves over bottom of unbaked pie crust; pour in egg mixture. Bake at 375 degrees for 15 minutes; reduce oven temperature to 350 degrees and bake an additional 25 minutes, or until the center is set. Cool completely on a wire rack. Serve with whipped topping. Serves 8.

Peggy Bowman
Palisade, CO

Turtle Pumpkin Pie

¼ c. plus 2 T. caramel ice-cream
   topping, divided
9-inch graham cracker crust
½ c. plus 2 T. pecan pieces,
   divided
1 c. milk
2 3.4-oz. pkgs. instant vanilla
   pudding mix
1 c. canned pumpkin
1 t. cinnamon
½ t. nutmeg
8-oz. container frozen whipped
   topping, thawed and divided

Pour ¼ cup caramel topping into crust; sprinkle with ½ cup nuts. In a large bowl, combine milk, dry pudding mixes, pumpkin and spices, whisking until well blended. Stir in 1 ½ cups whipped topping; spread mixture in crust. Chill at least one hour. Before serving, top with remaining whipped topping, drizzle with remaining caramel topping and sprinkle with remaining pecans. Serves 10.

Tonya Lewis-Holm
Scottsburg, IN

Chocolate-Raspberry Cream Pie

1 ½ c. chocolate wafers, crushed
3 T. butter, melted
2 c. whipping cream
½ c. sugar

1 t. vanilla extract
½ c. raspberry syrup
9-oz. pkg. chocolate wafers
¼ c. mini chocolate chips

Everyone loves the classic combination of chocolate and raspberry.

In a small bowl, combine crushed wafers and butter, stirring until blended; press into an ungreased 9" pie plate. Chill until firm. In a large bowl, beat whipping cream with an electric mixer at high speed until foamy; gradually add sugar and vanilla, continuing to beat until soft peaks form. Stir in raspberry syrup; spread a ½-inch-thick layer of whipped topping in bottom of pie crust. Top with ⅓ of wafers; repeat layers twice and finish with a layer of whipped topping. Cover and chill at least 12 hours. Sprinkle with chocolate chips before serving. Serves 8.

Shirley Heinlein
Upper Arlington, OH

freeze to please!

Make treats ahead of time and keep them frozen for last-minute gifts. Freeze pies for up to four months, breads for up to three months, cheesecakes for up to thirty days and baked, unfrosted cookies for up to six months. Be sure to freeze them in airtight, labeled and dated freezer-safe containers.

Molasses Chiffon Pie

Molasses Chiffon Pie

My mother always baked this special, sweet, old-fashioned pie for holidays and Sunday dinners.

—Eleanor

¼ c. cold water
1 T. unflavored gelatin
3 eggs
¾ c. light molasses
2 T. orange juice
½ t. cinnamon

⅛ t. salt
1 c. whipping cream
9-inch shortbread crumb crust
Optional: whipped topping, cinnamon

In a small bowl, combine cold water and gelatin; stir until gelatin dissolves. In a separate bowl, beat eggs with an electric mixer at medium speed until pale yellow in color; add molasses and beat until well blended. Pour molasses mixture into the top of a double boiler; cook over medium heat until thickened, stirring constantly. Remove from heat and add gelatin mixture, orange juice, cinnamon and salt, stirring well to blend. Chill until slightly thickened. In another bowl, beat cream with an electric mixer at high speed until stiff peaks form; fold into molasses mixture. Pour into crust and chill 4 hours, or until firm. Top each serving with whipped topping and cinnamon, if desired. Serves 6.

Eleanor Dionne
Beverly, MA

Caramel-Banana Pie

14-oz. can sweetened condensed
   milk
2 to 3 bananas, sliced
9-inch graham cracker pie crust
1 c. whipping cream
¼ c. powdered sugar
2 chocolate-covered toffee candy
   bars, chopped

Sweet, crunchy toffee makes this banana pie special.

Pour condensed milk into an 8" pie plate; cover with aluminum foil. Place covered pie plate in a shallow 2-quart casserole dish; pour hot water to a depth of ¼-inch into casserole dish. Bake at 425 degrees for one hour and 20 minutes, until milk is thick and caramel colored, adding more water to casserole dish if needed. Carefully remove casserole dish from oven; remove pie plate from casserole dish, uncover and set aside.

Place bananas on bottom of graham cracker crust; pour caramelized milk over bananas. Cool 30 minutes. In a medium bowl, beat cream with an electric mixer at high speed until foamy; gradually add powdered sugar, continuing to beat until stiff peaks form. Spread cream mixture over caramel layer. Chill at least 3 hours or overnight. Sprinkle with toffee candy bar bits before serving. Serves 8.

Dorthey Burgess
Mecosta, MI

Pear Pie

4 pears, peeled, cored and
   thinly sliced
3 T. frozen orange juice
   concentrate, thawed
9-inch pie crust
¾ c. all-purpose flour
½ c. sugar
⅓ c. butter
2 t. cinnamon, divided
⅛ t. salt

If you can, purchase locally grown pears... they'll likely be firmer and fresher than the imported varieties found in the supermarket.

In a large bowl, combine pears and orange juice and toss well; spoon pear mixture onto bottom of unbaked pie crust. In a medium bowl, combine flour, sugar, butter, one teaspoon cinnamon and salt. Mix until crumbly; sprinkle flour mixture over pear mixture. Sprinkle with remaining cinnamon. Bake at 400 degrees for 40 minutes, or until golden. Serves 8.

Shirley Heinlein
Upper Arlington, OH

Eggnog Pie

¼ c. cold water
1 T. unflavored gelatin
⅓ c. sugar
2 T. cornstarch
¼ t. salt
2 c. eggnog

1 t. vanilla extract
1 t. rum extract
2 c. whipping cream
9-inch graham cracker crust
Garnish: nutmeg

A perfect pick-me-up on a busy shopping day.

In a small bowl, combine cold water and gelatin; stir until gelatin dissolves. In a saucepan, combine sugar, cornstarch and salt, stirring to mix; add eggnog and stir until smooth. Bring to a boil over medium-low heat; cook 2 minutes, or until thickened, stirring constantly. Add gelatin mixture and stir until thoroughly blended. Remove from heat; cool to room temperature. Stir in extracts. In a separate bowl, beat cream with an electric mixer at high speed until soft peaks form; fold cream into gelatin mixture. Pour into pie crust. Cover and chill 4 hours, or until firm. Sprinkle top of pie with nutmeg. Serves 6 to 8.

Dale Duncan
Waterloo, IA

old-fashioned fun

Need a way to keep the kids busy while they're waiting for Santa's big day? Show them how to cut snowflakes from folded paper and then let them scatter a blizzard of snowflakes around the house...on the tree, down the banister, even taped to gift-wrapped packages.

SNIP
★
SNIP
★
SNIP

egghog
pie

Sour Cream-Apple Pie

to: Mrs. Wade

Sour Cream-Apple Pie

9-inch refrigerated pie crust
2 c. Rome apples, peeled, cored
    and chopped
1 c. sugar, divided
⅓ c. plus 2 T. all-purpose flour,
    divided
¼ t. salt
1 c. sour cream
1 egg, beaten
1 ½ t. vanilla extract
1 T. cinnamon
2 T. butter

The sour cream adds a touch of creaminess along with a slight tang to this classic apple pie.

Roll out crust and place in a 9" pie plate; place apples in bottom of pie crust. In a large bowl, combine ⅔ cup sugar, 2 tablespoons flour and salt; stir to mix. Add sour cream, egg and vanilla; beat with an electric mixer at medium speed until smooth. Pour mixture over apples. Bake at 425 degrees for 15 minutes; reduce heat to 350 degrees and bake an additional 30 minutes. In a small bowl, combine cinnamon, butter, remaining flour and remaining sugar; sprinkle on top of pie. Increase heat to 400 degrees and bake an additional 10 minutes. Serves 8.

Lois Vardaro
East Northport, NY

Apple-Gingerbread Cobbler

14-oz. pkg. gingerbread cake mix,
    divided
¾ c. water
¼ c. brown sugar, packed
½ c. butter, divided
½ c. chopped pecans
2 21-oz. cans apple pie filling

In a medium bowl, combine 2 cups gingerbread mix and water; stir until smooth. In a separate bowl, combine remaining gingerbread mix and brown sugar, stirring to mix; cut in ¼ cup butter until mixture is crumbly. Stir in pecans; set aside. In a large saucepan, combine pie filling and remaining butter; cook over medium heat for 5 minutes, or until thoroughly heated, stirring often. Spoon apple mixture evenly into a lightly greased 11"x 7" baking pan. Spoon gingerbread mixture over apple mixture; sprinkle with pecan mixture. Bake at 375 degrees for 30 to 35 minutes, until center is set. Serves 8.

Wendy Jacobs
Idaho Falls, ID

TO
JULIE

The Sweetest Spoons and
Candy Tea Stirrers, page 107

Cheery Sips & Stirs

For the beverage drinkers on your list, our tasty selection of seasonal favorites is sure to please.

Chocolate Eggnog

A great no-fuss recipe for jazzing up store-bought eggnog.

2 qts. eggnog
16-oz. can chocolate syrup
Optional: ½ c. light rum

1 c. whipping cream
2 T. powdered sugar
Garnish: baking cocoa

Combine eggnog, chocolate syrup and rum, if desired, in a large punch bowl, stirring well. In a separate bowl, beat whipping cream with an electric mixer at high speed until foamy. Add powdered sugar and continue beating until stiff peaks form. Dollop whipped cream over eggnog; sift cocoa over top. Serve immediately. Makes 3 quarts.

Valarie Dennard
Palatka, FL

Creamy Cocoa 3 Ways

When the weather turns damp and chilly, I like to have sweet hot cocoa ready and waiting when the kids arrive home from school. This slow-cooker recipe makes it so easy, even on the busiest day!

–Linda

¾ c. sugar
½ c. baking cocoa
2 qts. milk

1 T. vanilla extract
Garnish: whipped cream or marshmallows

Combine sugar and cocoa in a slow cooker; stir in milk. Cover and cook on low setting 3 to 4 hours. Just before serving, stir in vanilla. Using a whisk, hand mixer or an immersion blender, carefully beat until frothy. Ladle hot cocoa into mugs. Garnish with whipped cream or marshmallows. Makes 8 to 10 servings.

Nice & Spicy Cocoa: Along with the cocoa, add one teaspoon cinnamon and ⅛ teaspoon nutmeg to the milk. Cover and cook as directed.

Mocha Cocoa: Prepare the recipe as directed. Before serving, add ¾ teaspoon instant coffee granules to each mug of hot cocoa; stir to mix.

Linda Robson
Boston, MA

true country charm

Decorate the top of pine cones with berries, nuts, raffia and other natural items. Hang or pile them in a basket...so easy!

Chocolate Eggnog

White Hot Chocolate

Use whole milk for the richest flavor.

6-oz. pkg. white chocolate chips
½ to 1 t. cinnamon
Optional: ¼ t. cayenne pepper

1 egg, beaten
3 ¼ c. milk, divided
Optional: additional cinnamon

In a large saucepan, bring water to a simmer and reduce heat. Place chocolate chips in a large metal bowl and place bowl over pan of barely simmering water, stirring until chips melt. Stir in cinnamon and cayenne pepper, if desired; whisk in egg until smooth. Gradually add one cup milk and whisk 2 minutes, or until blended. Stir in remaining milk; increase heat and cook until mixture is hot but not boiling. Ladle into mugs; sprinkle with additional cinnamon, if desired. Serves 4.

Geneva Rogers
Gillette, WY

Buttermint Coffee Blend

½ c. powdered non-dairy creamer
½ c. buttermints, coarsely
  crushed
¼ c. powdered sugar

2 c. powdered milk
¾ c. instant coffee granules,
  divided
2 1-pt. wide-mouth jars with lids

Combine creamer, buttermints, sugar and milk in a medium bowl, stirring to mix; divide mixture evenly between jars. Layer half of instant coffee on top of creamer mixture in each jar. Secure lids and attach instructions. Makes 2 jars.

Marj Miller
Tyler, TX

Instructions: Place Buttermint Coffee Blend in a bowl and toss lightly; spoon mixture back into jar. Combine ¼ cup mix with ⅔ cup boiling water in a mug; stir until mixture dissolves. Makes one serving.

clever gift tags

Dress up Buttermint Coffee Blend gift tags with coffee beans. Just arrange the beans as a border or in a design, or use them to spell out names.

South Sea Tea Blend

For a cool hot-weather gift, place a container of this mix into a pitcher with instructions for making sun tea!

2 c. unsweetened instant tea
1 3-oz. bx. orange gelatin mix
1 3-oz. bx. pineapple gelatin mix
1 c. sugar
¾ t. coconut extract
⅛ t. vanilla powder

Combine all ingredients in a food processor; process until well blended. Place in an airtight container and attach instructions. Makes 3 ½ cups.

Tara Horton
Delaware, OH

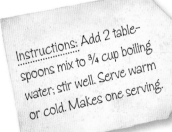

Instructions: Add 2 table-spoons mix to ¾ cup boiling water; stir well. Serve warm or cold. Makes one serving.

Holiday Wassail

It's our family tradition to enjoy wassail while we open presents Christmas morning. The citrus-spice aroma fills the house and really puts us in the holiday mood!

—Tara

3 qts. apple juice
2 ¼ c. pineapple juice
2 c. orange juice
½ c. sugar
3-inch cinnamon stick
1 t. whole cloves

Combine all ingredients in a large saucepan. Cover and place over medium-low heat; simmer 30 minutes. Uncover and simmer an additional 30 minutes. Strain mixture and discard spices. Serves 10 to 12.

Tara Horton
Delaware, OH

Apricot-Apple Cider

Just as the trees begin to show off their radiant autumn colors and there's a chill in the air, I look forward to serving this warm and cozy harvest brew in my home and country store. I've shared many copies of this recipe!

—Kelly

1 gal. apple cider
11 ½ oz. can apricot nectar
1 c. sugar
2 c. orange juice
¾ c. lemon juice
4 4-inch cinnamon sticks
2 t. allspice
1 t. ground cloves
½ t. nutmeg

In a large stockpot, combine all ingredients and bring to a boil over medium heat. Reduce heat and simmer at least 10 minutes. Makes about 20 servings.

Kelly Gillow
Easton, PA

Christmas Snow Punch

Children will love the "snow" on top!

1-ltr. bottle red fruit punch, chilled
2-ltr. bottle lemon-lime soda, chilled
½ gal. vanilla ice cream

In a large punch bowl, combine punch and soda, stirring to mix. Scoop ice cream into round balls and float on top of punch. Serve immediately. Serves 15 to 20.

Connie Herek
Bay City, MI

pretty & tasty spoons

Wrap chocolate-covered spoons with clear cellophane, gather the ends and tie; add a festive ribbon at the end of the bowl of the spoon. Fill a tin or china cup with coffee beans and insert the spoons, handles down, so the spoons stand up in the beans for a fun presentation.

The Sweetest Spoons

pictured on page 100

1 c. chocolate chips
¼ c. butterscotch chips
⅛ t. shortening

20 plastic spoons
Optional: colorful sprinkles

Microwave chocolate chips in a microwave-safe bowl on high for 1 minute, or until melted and smooth, stirring after 30 seconds. Place butterscotch chips and shortening in a plastic zipping bag; seal bag. Microwave on high 30 seconds; squeeze bag until butterscotch melts. Using scissors, snip a tiny hole in one corner of bag. Dip the spoons into melted chocolate, covering the bowl of each spoon; place spoons on wax paper and chill until firm. Drizzle chocolate-covered spoons with melted butterscotch. Place spoons on wax paper and sprinkle with colorful sprinkles, if desired. Chill until firm and then wrap each spoon individually in plastic wrap. Makes 20.

Be sure to use sturdy plastic spoons; lesser-quality ones don't hold up well when stirred into hot liquids.

Candy Tea Stirrers

pictured on page 100

½ c. fruit-flavored hard candy, crushed

½ c. corn syrup
24 plastic spoons

Line a 15"x10" jelly-roll pan with wax paper; spray with non-stick vegetable spray. In batches, combine 2 tablespoons desired crushed candy flavor and 2 tablespoons corn syrup in a heavy saucepan; cook over low heat until candy melts, stirring frequently. Spoon mixture into the bowl of each spoon; place spoons on prepared pan with the handles on the rim so the assorted spoon bowls are level. Cool until mixture hardens. Store in an airtight container. Makes 24.

Wrap each spoon in cellophane and tie to a container of tea mix.

Rogene Rogers
Bemidji, MN

Mini Butterscotch Drop
Scones, page 123

Best-Ever Muffins & Breads

Fresh-from-the-oven baked goods deliver on taste and presentation...you can almost smell them now!

Cranberry-Pecan-Coconut Loaf

It's so nice to have this on hand when friends and family stop by for a quick visit.

2 c. all-purpose flour
2 t. baking powder
1 t. salt
1 c. butter, softened
1 c. sugar
3 eggs
2 t. vanilla extract
⅔ c. milk
1 ½ c. cranberries
¾ c. pecans, coarsely chopped
½ c. sweetened flaked coconut

In a large bowl, combine flour, baking powder and salt; stir and set aside. Combine butter, sugar, eggs and vanilla in a separate large bowl; mix well with an electric mixer at low speed. Add flour mixture to butter mixture alternately with milk, beginning and ending with flour mixture; mix just until blended. Fold in cranberries, pecans and coconut; spread in 4 greased 8"x4" mini loaf pans. Bake at 350 degrees for one hour and 45 to 50 minutes, until a toothpick inserted in center comes out clean. Cool completely in pans on wire racks. Makes 4 loaves.

Diana Pindell
Wooster, OH

Holiday Eggnog Bread

This was one of the first things that I ever made. I baked my first loaf when I was 12, and I make it for my family often during the holidays. Since everyone likes it so much, I make it as long as the grocery store sells eggnog!
—Summer

2 eggs, beaten
1 c. sugar
1 c. eggnog
½ c. butter, melted and
    slightly cooled
1 t. vanilla extract
2 ¼ c. all-purpose flour
2 ¼ t. nutmeg
2 t. baking powder

In a large bowl, combine eggs, sugar, eggnog, butter and vanilla; blend well. Add remaining ingredients; stir until moistened. Lightly grease the bottom of a 9"x5" loaf pan; pour batter into pan. Bake at 350 degrees for 35 to 45 minutes, until a toothpick inserted in center comes out clean. Cool in pan on a wire rack for 10 minutes. Remove from pan. Cool completely on wire rack before slicing. Makes one loaf.

Summer Staib
Broomfield, CO

Cranberry-Pecan-Coconut Loaf

Velvet Pumpkin Bread

This makes the best quick bread...sifting is the secret.

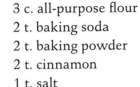

3 c. all-purpose flour
2 t. baking soda
2 t. baking powder
2 t. cinnamon
1 t. salt

2 c. sugar
1 ½ c. oil
4 eggs, well beaten
2 c. canned pumpkin

Sift together flour, baking soda, baking powder, cinnamon and salt. Combine sugar and oil in a separate large bowl and mix well; blend flour mixture into sugar mixture. Add eggs and pumpkin; mix well. Pour into 2 greased 9"x5" loaf pans; bake at 350 degrees for one hour, or until a toothpick inserted in center comes out clean. Cool completely in pans on wire racks. Makes 2 loaves.

Toni LePrevost
Parma, OH

Garlic Bubble Bread

This flavorful dinner version of Monkey Bread is super easy to make! Whenever I serve it, someone asks for the recipe.

—Joanne

16-oz. frozen bread dough, thawed
¼ c. butter, melted
1 T. dried parsley

1 t. garlic powder
½ t. garlic salt
Optional: sesame or poppy seed

Cut dough into one-inch pieces. Combine butter, parsley, garlic power and garlic salt in a small bowl. Dip dough pieces into butter mixture to coat; layer in a buttered 9"x5" loaf pan. Sprinkle sesame or poppy seed over the top, if desired. Cover dough with plastic wrap; let rise in a warm place (85 degrees), free from drafts, until double in bulk (about one hour). Bake at 350 degrees for 30 minutes, or until golden. Cool completely in pan on a wire rack. Makes 4 to 6 servings.

Joanne Grosskopf
Lake in the Hills, IL

Rosemary & Onion Bread

16-oz. frozen bread dough, thawed
1 to 2 T. olive oil
1 to 2 t. dried rosemary
¼ c. chopped onion

Coat dough with oil; place on a lightly greased baking sheet. Press rosemary and onion into dough. Bake at 350 degrees for 30 to 40 minutes, until golden. Serves 6.

Donna Clement
Latham, NY

My mother used to bake this bread every Sunday. I can almost smell it now...mmm!

–Donna

Mini Cheddar Loaves

2 ½ c. shredded Cheddar cheese
3 ½ c. biscuit baking mix
2 eggs, beaten
1 ¼ c. milk

In a large bowl, combine cheese and biscuit mix. Combine eggs and milk in a separate bowl and beat well; stir egg mixture into cheese mixture. Pour into 2 greased 7"x4" loaf pans. Bake at 350 degrees for 40 to 55 minutes, until a toothpick inserted in center comes out clean. Cool completely in pans on wire racks. Makes 2 loaves.

Mary King
Ashville, AL

old is new

Turn old glass ornaments into shiny new ones with gold or silver glitter paint. Hand them out to guests with a sweet treat as a party gift.

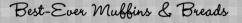

Cranberry Upside-Down Muffins

Served warm, these tangy muffins taste delicious alongside savory soups and stews.

2 ½ c. all-purpose flour
½ c. sugar
1 T. baking powder
½ t. salt

1 ¼ c. milk
⅓ c. butter, melted and slightly
    cooled
1 egg, beaten

In a large bowl, combine flour, sugar, baking powder and salt; blend well. Add milk, butter and egg to flour mixture; stir just until moistened. Prepare Cranberry Topping; spoon topping into 18 greased muffin cups. Spoon batter over topping, filling each cup ⅔ full. Bake at 400 degrees for 20 to 25 minutes, until a toothpick inserted in center comes out clean. Immediately invert onto a wire rack placed on wax paper; serve warm. Makes 1 ½ dozen.

Cranberry Topping

⅓ c. brown sugar, packed
¼ c. butter
½ t. cinnamon

½ c. cranberries, halved
½ c. chopped nuts

Combine all ingredients in a small saucepan. Cook over medium heat until brown sugar dissolves. Cool 10 minutes.

Barbara Girlardo
Pittsburgh, PA

Butter-Rum Muffins

⅔ c. butter, softened
1⅓ c. sugar
4 eggs
4 c. all-purpose flour
2 T. baking powder

¼ t. salt
2 c. milk
1 t. butter flavoring
1 t. rum extract
11-oz. pkg. butterscotch chips

In a large bowl, combine butter, sugar and eggs; beat with an electric mixer at medium speed until well blended. In a separate bowl, stir together flour, baking powder and salt. Stir together milk and flavorings. Add milk mixture to butter mixture alternately with flour mixture; stir well. Fold in chips. Fill lightly greased muffin cups ⅔ full. Bake at 350 degrees for 15 to 20 minutes, until a toothpick inserted in center comes out clean. Makes 3 dozen.

Diana Krol
Nickerson, KS

Emma's Gingerbread
Muffins

Emma's Gingerbread Muffins

½ c. butter, softened
½ c. shortening
¾ c. sugar
3 eggs
¼ c. golden or light corn syrup
½ c. molasses

3 c. all-purpose flour
2 t. cinnamon
2 t. ground ginger
1 t. nutmeg
1 t. baking soda
1 c. buttermilk

These muffins are very moist and spicy. You won't be able to eat just one!

In a large bowl, combine butter and shortening. Beat with an electric mixer at medium speed until creamy. Add sugar; beat just until combined. Add eggs, one at a time; beat after each addition. Add corn syrup and molasses; beat just until blended. Sift together flour and spices. Dissolve baking soda in buttermilk; add soda mixture to butter mixture alternately with flour mixture, stirring just until combined. Fill greased and floured muffin cups ⅔ full. Bake at 350 degrees for 15 minutes, or until a toothpick inserted in center comes out clean. Makes 2 ½ dozen.

Bernadette Dobias
Houston, TX

Marie's Yeast Rolls

Chocolatey Banana Muffins

2 c. all-purpose flour
⅓ c. sugar
2 T. baking cocoa
1 T. baking powder

1 c. bananas, mashed
⅔ c. oil
1 egg
1 c. semi-sweet chocolate chips

Try making these muffins with chunks of chocolate bars instead of chips...bigger bites of chocolate are sure to please.

Stir together flour, sugar, cocoa and baking powder in a bowl. In a separate bowl, combine bananas, oil and egg; beat with an electric mixer at medium speed until blended. Gradually add flour mixture to banana mixture, stirring just until blended. Fold in chocolate chips; fill paper-lined muffin cups ¾ full. Bake at 425 degrees for 15 to 20 minutes, until a toothpick inserted in center comes out clean; remove from pan and cool completely on a wire rack. Makes one dozen.

Diana Pindell
Wooster, OH

Marie's Yeast Rolls

1 env. active dry yeast
2 c. very warm water
½ c. butter, melted

¼ c. sugar
1 egg, beaten
4 c. self-rising flour

You can refrigerate this batter in an airtight container for up to two weeks...so convenient!

In a large bowl, dissolve yeast in very warm water (110 to 115 degrees). Add remaining ingredients; stir well. Fill well-greased muffin cups ¾ full. Bake at 425 degrees for 20 minutes, or until golden. Makes 3 dozen.

Marie Stewart
Pensacola, FL

Sunday Dinner Potato Rolls

2 env. active dry yeast
2 c. very warm water
½ c. sugar
1 ¼ T. salt
1 c. warm mashed potatoes

½ c. butter, softened
2 eggs, beaten
7 ½ c. all-purpose flour, divided
3 T. butter, melted

In a large bowl, dissolve yeast in very warm water (110 to 115 degrees). Add sugar, salt, potatoes, butter and eggs; blend well. Gradually add 3 ½ cups flour, beating with an electric mixer at medium speed; continue beating for 2 minutes. Gradually stir in remaining flour.

Turn dough out onto a floured surface and knead until smooth and elastic (about 10 minutes). Brush dough with melted butter; place in a bowl, cover with plastic wrap and chill 2 hours. Punch down dough; cover with plastic wrap and refrigerate overnight. Punch down dough and knead lightly 4 or 5 times. Divide dough in half; shape each half into 24 rolls.

Place rolls on lightly greased baking sheets; cover and let rise in a warm place (85 degrees), free from drafts, for one hour, or until double in bulk. Bake at 325 degrees for 40 minutes, or until golden. Makes 4 dozen.

Mary Murray
Mount Vernon, OH

When I was growing up, Sunday dinner was the most important meal in our home. These rolls were always served fresh from the oven.

—Mary

Stone-Ground Corn Rolls

2 c. milk
¾ c. cornmeal
½ c. sugar
½ c. shortening
1 ½ t. salt

1 env. active dry yeast
¼ c. very warm water
2 eggs, beaten
6 c. all-purpose flour

In a large saucepan, combine milk and cornmeal; cook over medium heat 15 minutes, or until mixture thickens, stirring frequently. Remove from heat; add sugar, shortening and salt and stir until blended. Cool slightly. Dissolve yeast in very warm water (110 to 115 degrees). Add eggs and yeast mixture to milk mixture, stirring to blend; gradually stir in flour. Place dough on a lightly floured surface and knead until smooth, about 5 minutes. Shape dough into 2-inch balls; arrange dough balls 2 inches apart on a greased baking sheet. Cover and let rise in a warm place (85 degrees), free from drafts, for one hour, or until double in bulk. Bake at 375 degrees for 15 minutes, or until golden. Makes one dozen.

Tina Goodpasture
Meadowview, VA

Mary's Sweet Corn Cake

½ c. butter, softened
⅓ c. masa harina
¼ c. water
10-oz. pkg. frozen corn, thawed
⅓ c. sugar

3 T. yellow cornmeal
2 T. whipping cream
¼ t. baking powder
¼ t. salt

In a large bowl, beat butter with an electric mixer at medium speed until creamy. Gradually beat in flour; beat in water and set aside. Place corn in a food processor or blender. Pulse to chop corn coarsely; stir chopped corn into butter mixture. Combine sugar and remaining ingredients in a separate bowl; stir until well blended. Stir sugar mixture into butter mixture. Pour into a lightly greased 8"x8" baking pan; cover pan with aluminum foil. Set pan into a 13"x9" baking pan; add water one-third of the way up around smaller pan. Bake at 350 degrees for 50 to 60 minutes, until a toothpick inserted in center comes out clean. Uncover smaller pan; let stand for 15 minutes. Scoop out servings with a small scoop; serve warm. Serves 8.

Mary Murray
Mount Vernon, OH

Do not substitute cornmeal or regular corn flour for the masa harina in this recipe... you will not get the same results because it is processed from a different type of corn.

Auntie Kay Kay's Sticky Buns

2 16-oz. pkgs. frozen sweet bread
    dough
½ c. cinnamon-sugar
½ c. butter

½ c. sugar
½ c. brown sugar, packed
½ c. vanilla ice cream

Place frozen bread dough in a lightly greased 13"x9" baking pan. Cover pan with plastic wrap sprayed with non-stick vegetable spray; thaw dough in the refrigerator overnight. Remove thawed dough from pan and cut into bite-size pieces; roll each piece in cinnamon-sugar to coat. Place coated dough pieces in pan. Melt butter, sugars and ice cream in a saucepan over medium-low heat; stir until smooth. Pour butter mixture over coated dough pieces. Bake at 400 degrees for 20 minutes. Serves 6 to 8.

Jen Sell
Farmington, MN

Everyone loves having my Auntie Kay Kay visit! She always starts making these sticky buns the day before so they are ready to bake the next morning.

—Jen

Orange-Glazed Chocolate Rolls

3 c. all-purpose flour, divided
2 env. active dry yeast
1 t. salt
1 t. cinnamon
1 ¼ c. water

⅓ c. sugar
⅓ c. butter
1 egg
Optional: ½ c. raisins
1 c. semi-sweet chocolate chips

In a large bowl, stir together 1 ½ cups flour, yeast, salt and cinnamon. Combine water, sugar and butter in a saucepan over medium-low heat, stirring constantly until butter is almost melted (115 to 120 degrees). Add sugar mixture to flour mixture; blend until smooth. Mix in egg; stir in remaining flour. Fold in raisins, if desired; cover dough and let rise in a warm place (85 degrees), free from drafts, for one hour, or until double in bulk. Punch down dough; let rest for 10 minutes. Fold in chocolate chips; fill greased muffin cups ⅔ full. Cover; let rise until double in bulk. Bake at 425 degrees for 10 to 15 minutes, until golden; remove from pan and cool completely. Drizzle with Glaze before serving. Makes about 1½ dozen.

Glaze

½ c. powdered sugar   3 t. orange juice

Combine sugar and juice in a small bowl; stir until smooth and creamy.

Geneva Rogers
Gillette, WY

girls night in

Get together with girlfriends for a Christmas craft night. Ask each friend to bring along an idea and the supplies to share. It's such fun to make gift tags, bath fizzies and ornaments together!

Golden Raisin Buns

Golden Raisin Buns

1 c. water
½ c. butter
1 t. sugar
¼ t. salt

1 c. all-purpose flour
4 eggs
½ c. golden raisins

When you need a little something sweet, these will hit the spot.

In a large saucepan, combine water, butter, sugar and salt and bring to a boil over high heat. Remove from heat; add flour, stirring until mixture pulls away from sides of pan. Add eggs, one at a time, beating well after each addition. Stir in raisins. Drop by heaping tablespoonfuls onto an ungreased baking sheet; bake at 375 degrees for 30 minutes, or until golden. Makes 2 dozen.

Sharon Hoskins
Warrensburg, MO

One-Bowl Cheddar
Biscuits

One-Bowl Cheddar Biscuits

These biscuits whip up oh–so quickly...and they'll be eaten even quicker!

2 ¼ c. biscuit baking mix
½ c. shredded Cheddar cheese
2 T. fresh parsley, chopped
¼ c. sour cream

2 T. Dijon mustard
⅓ c. milk
1 egg, beaten

In a large bowl, combine baking mix, cheese and parsley; stir just until blended. In a small bowl, combine sour cream, mustard and milk; stir well. Add sour cream mixture to baking mix mixture, stirring just until blended. Place dough on a lightly floured surface; knead 10 times. Pat dough into a ½-inch-thick circle; cut with a 2-inch biscuit cutter. Arrange biscuits on ungreased baking sheets; brush tops lightly with beaten egg. Bake at 425 degrees for 12 to 15 minutes, until golden. Serve warm. Makes 3 dozen.

Christine Schnaufer
Geneseo, IL

Cream Biscuits

2 c. all-purpose flour
1 T. baking powder
3 T. sugar
½ t. salt
1 ¼ c. whipping cream
milk

In a large bowl, combine flour, baking powder, sugar and salt; stir well. Gradually add cream, stirring until mixture forms a soft dough. Shape dough into a ball. Knead dough 6 times on a lightly floured surface; roll out to ⅓-inch thickness. Cut dough into circles with the rim of a glass and place on an ungreased baking sheet. Brush tops of biscuits with milk; bake at 425 degrees for 10 to 15 minutes, until golden. Makes one dozen.

Jodi Bielawski
Manchester, NH

Baskets of warm biscuits, bowls of soup and the company of friends will complete any dinner table.

Mini Butterscotch Drop Scones

pictured on page 108

2 c. all-purpose flour
½ c. brown sugar, packed
2 t. baking powder
¼ t. salt
⅓ c. butter, softened
1 c. butterscotch chips
½ c. pecans, toasted and chopped
1 egg, beaten
⅔ c. whipping cream
½ t. vanilla extract
Optional: powdered sugar

In a large bowl, combine flour, brown sugar, baking powder and salt, stirring until blended. Cut in butter with a pastry blender or 2 knives until fine crumbs form. Stir in chips and nuts. In a separate bowl, combine egg, cream and vanilla, whisking until well mixed. Add egg mixture to flour mixture, stirring just until moistened. Drop by rounded tablespoonfuls onto parchment paper-lined baking sheets. Bake at 375 degrees for 12 to 15 minutes, until golden. Remove from pans and cool on wire racks. Sprinkle with powdered sugar, if desired. Makes 3 dozen.

Margaret Welder
Madrid, IA

My husband loves scones, so my recipe file has many different scone recipes, most of them rolled and cut into wedges. This recipe is a bit different, however, because it makes drop scones, and the butterscotch chips and nuts make them sweet.
—Margaret

special door prize

Set a basket of muffins on a secret pal's doorstep and hang a small daisy chain wreath from the doorknob...it's so much fun to keep them guessing!

Cozy Soups & More

Deliver a thoughtful gift of home-cooked comfort with these easy & delicious recipes for a great pick-me-up.

Herbed Chicken-Barley Soup,
page 128

Slow-Cooker Spicy Chili

This slow-cooker recipe is similar to a popular fast-food chili recipe. We love to serve it spooned over baked potatoes and topped with shredded cheese.

1 lb. ground beef, browned
   and drained
16-oz. can red kidney beans,
   drained and rinsed
10½-oz. can French onion soup
6-oz. can tomato paste
4-oz. can diced green chiles
¾ c. water
1 T. chili powder
2 t. ground cumin
½ t. pepper
⅛ to ¼ t. hot pepper sauce
Garnish: shredded Cheddar
   cheese

Add all ingredients except garnish in a 5-quart slow cooker; stir to blend. Cover and cook on low setting for 4 to 6 hours. Spoon into serving bowls and garnish with cheese. Serves 6 to 8.

Lisa Sett
Thousand Oaks, CA

Cider Mill Stew

3 T. all-purpose flour
1 t. salt
½ t. pepper
1 lb. stew beef cubes
2 T. oil
1 c. apple cider
1 c. water
1 c. beef broth
1 T. cider vinegar
½ t. dried thyme
2 carrots, peeled and cut into
   1-inch pieces
1 stalk celery, cut into 1-inch
   pieces
1 potato, peeled and cubed
1 onion, sliced

Combine flour, salt and pepper in a large plastic zipping bag. Add beef in batches; shake to coat. Brown beef in hot oil, in batches, in a Dutch oven; drain. Stir in cider, water, broth, vinegar and thyme; bring to a boil over medium heat. Reduce heat; cover and simmer for one hour and 45 minutes, or until meat is tender. Add vegetables; return to a boil. Reduce heat; cover and simmer for 30 minutes, or until vegetables are tender. Serves 4.

Laura Lett
Delaware, OH

Slow-Cooker Spicy Chili

Herbed Chicken-Barley Soup

pictured on page 124

Mmm...there's nothing better than homemade chicken soup!

3 to 4 lbs. chicken
8 c. water
1½ c. carrots, diced
1 c. celery, diced
½ c. onion, chopped
½ c. pearled barley, uncooked
1 cube chicken bouillon
1 bay leaf
1 t. salt
½ t. poultry seasoning
½ t. dried sage
½ t. pepper

Combine chicken and water in a large stockpot over medium heat; cook until chicken is tender and juices run clear when pierced with a fork. Remove chicken and cool slightly; reserve broth. Allow broth to cool; skim off fat. Shred chicken, discarding bones and skin. Return chicken to broth in kettle along with remaining ingredients. Cover; simmer over low heat for at least one hour, or until vegetables and barley are tender. Discard bay leaf. Serves 6 to 8.

Janet Allen
Hauser, ID

Roast Chicken-Corn Tortilla Soup

Garnish with quick-fried strips of red corn tortillas.

1 deli-roast chicken, cut into
    bite-size pieces
4 c. chicken broth
½ c. chipotle salsa
½ c. tequila lime salsa
1 to 2 c. corn tortilla chips, crushed
juice of ½ lime
½ c. fresh cilantro, chopped
salt and pepper to taste
Optional: shredded Cheddar
    cheese, sour cream, fried
    tortilla strips

Combine chicken, broth and salsas in a large saucepan over medium-high heat. Add tortilla chips and simmer for 10 minutes. Stir in lime juice, cilantro, salt and pepper. Serve immediately; top with cheese, sour cream and tortilla strips, if desired. Serves 4.

Sherry Noble
Kennett, MO

packaged with love

Send home a container of hearty homemade soup with a college student or older person who lives alone...a heartfelt gesture that will be much appreciated.

Tom Turkey Noodle Soup

2 18½-oz. cans turkey broth
4⅔ c. water
1 T. dried parsley

1 t. dried, minced onion
4 c. cooked turkey, diced
8-oz. pkg. egg noodles, uncooked

Combine broth, water, parsley and onion in a large stockpot over medium heat; bring to a boil. Add turkey and noodles; reduce heat and simmer for 10 to 15 minutes. Serves 4 to 6.

Emily Edwards
Alliance, OH

Turkey & Dressing Soup

2½ lb. turkey breast
10 c. water
2 carrots, peeled and chopped
3 c. celery, chopped and divided
2 onions, chopped and divided
2 bay leaves

1 t. salt
½ t. pepper
1½ t. dried sage
1 t. poultry seasoning
Garnish: 2 eggs, hardboiled, peeled and sliced

Combine turkey, water, carrots, 2 cups celery, one onion and bay leaves in a Dutch oven. Season with salt and pepper. Bring to a boil over medium-high heat; reduce heat and simmer 1½ hours. Remove turkey; set aside. When cool enough to handle, remove meat from bones and chop; discard skin. Strain broth and discard vegetables; return to Dutch oven with chopped turkey. Stir in remaining celery, onion and seasonings; bring to a boil. Reduce heat and simmer, uncovered, 45 minutes. Garnish with egg slices. Serves 10 to 12.

Cathy Garrett
Balch Springs, TX

In the past, I've used chicken breast in place of turkey...it's really tasty with either one. My family loves this soup, especially with warm cornbread.
—Cathy

Kielbasa-Cabbage Soup

My son-in-law came up with this dish. It's so easy and very tasty... real stick-to-your-ribs food on a cold winter day!

—Karen

1 lb. Kielbasa sausage ring, halved and sliced into ¼-inch pieces
28-oz. can stewed tomatoes
2 15½-oz. cans dark red kidney beans, drained and rinsed
½ head cabbage, chopped
1 c. onion, diced
1 c. carrot, peeled and diced
1 t. pepper
6 to 8 c. chicken broth
½ t. dried parsley
½ t. dried thyme
½ t. dried oregano

Combine Kielbasa sausage, vegetables and pepper in a large stockpot; add broth to cover. Bring to a boil over medium heat; cook for 20 minutes. Reduce heat to low and continue cooking for 30 minutes, stirring occasionally. Stir in herbs just before serving. Serves 8 to 10.

Karen McCann
Marion, OH

Slow-Cooked Hearty Pork Stew

1 ½ lbs. boneless pork shoulder, cubed
1 lb. Kielbasa sausage ring, sliced
14½-oz. can chicken broth
2 c. onion, chopped
6 carrots, peeled and thickly sliced
2 cloves garlic, minced
2 15-oz. cans cannellini beans, drained and rinsed
3 T. tomato paste
1 t. dried thyme
½ t. pepper
14½-oz. can diced tomatoes, drained
Optional: Crumb Topping

Combine all ingredients except tomatoes and Crumb Topping in a 5-quart slow cooker. Cover and cook on low setting for 8 to 10 hours, or on high setting for 4 to 5 hours. Stir in tomatoes; cover and cook an additional 10 minutes. If using Crumb Topping, place stew in a lightly greased, shallow, 3-quart casserole dish. Sprinkle with Crumb Topping; bake at 400 degrees for 15 to 20 minutes, until topping is crisp and golden. Serves 8.

Crumb Topping

1 ½ c. soft bread crumbs
¼ c. fresh parsley, chopped
¼ c. grated Parmesan cheese
2 T. olive oil

Combine all ingredients in a large bowl and toss well.

Audrey Lett
Newark, DE

Kielbasa-Cabbage
Soup

Crawfish-Corn Chowder

This creamy chowder has just the right amount of spice. If you like more spice, bump up the hot pepper sauce.

12-oz. pkg. bacon, crisply cooked, crumbled and drippings reserved
2 c. potatoes, peeled and diced
1 c. onion, diced
2 T. butter
2 pts. half-and-half
2 16-oz. cans creamed corn
1 T. Creole seasoning
Optional: 1 t. hot pepper sauce
1 lb. frozen crawfish tails or uncooked medium shrimp, peeled

Heat 4 tablespoons reserved drippings in a large stockpot. Cook potatoes and onion in hot drippings, stirring occasionally, for 15 minutes, or until golden. Stir in butter, half-and-half, corn, seasoning and hot sauce, if desired. Cook over medium heat 20 to 30 minutes, until potatoes are tender. Add crawfish or shrimp and simmer for an additonal 4 to 6 minutes. Sprinkle each serving with crumbled bacon. Serves 6 to 8.

Becky Garrett
Richardson, TX

Holiday Best Oyster Stew

½ c. butter
1 c. celery, chopped
1 c. onion, chopped
7-oz. can sliced mushrooms, drained
1 pt. oysters, undrained
10 ¾-oz. can cream of potato soup
4 c. milk
1 pt. half-and-half
1 t. salt
1 t. pepper
Garnish: paprika or dried parsley

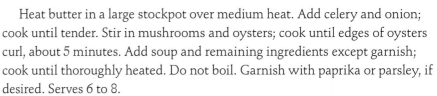

Heat butter in a large stockpot over medium heat. Add celery and onion; cook until tender. Stir in mushrooms and oysters; cook until edges of oysters curl, about 5 minutes. Add soup and remaining ingredients except garnish; cook until thoroughly heated. Do not boil. Garnish with paprika or parsley, if desired. Serves 6 to 8.

Teresa Stiegelmeyer
Indianapolis, IN

Crawfish-Corn Chowder

cozy winter feast

Invite friends over for a Soup Supper on a frosty winter evening. Everyone can bring their favorite soup or bread to share...you provide the bowls, spoons and a crackling fire!

Cauliflower-Cheddar Soup

2 T. butter
½ c. onion, chopped
3 c. cauliflower, coarsely chopped
10 ½-oz. can chicken broth

2½ c. milk
¼ c. all-purpose flour
1 ½ c. shredded Cheddar cheese
salt and pepper to taste

Melt butter in a large saucepan over medium heat; add onion and sauté until tender. Stir in cauliflower and broth; bring to a boil. Reduce heat; cover and simmer for 12 to 15 minutes, until cauliflower is tender. Whisk together milk and flour until smooth; add to saucepan. Cook and stir over medium-high heat until thickened. Remove from heat; add cheese and stir until melted. Add salt and pepper to taste. Serves 4.

Stacey Laliberty
Ontario, Canada

Chunky Minestrone

This recipe has been a huge hit at soup luncheons, family gatherings and work. It's easy to make and low calorie for calorie watchers. We all just love it and hope you will too!

—Sharon

1 T. olive oil
1 ½ c. onion, chopped
1 carrot, peeled and sliced
2 cloves garlic, minced
14 ½-oz. can diced tomatoes
4 c. chicken broth
1 c. water
1 t. Italian seasoning

½ c. long-cooking rice or soup pasta, uncooked
15-oz. can kidney beans, drained and rinsed
1 zucchini, chopped
½ t. pepper
Garnish: grated Parmesan cheese

Heat oil in a Dutch oven over medium heat. Add onion, carrot and garlic; cook for 3 minutes, or until tender. Stir in tomatoes with juice, broth, water, seasoning and uncooked rice or pasta. Bring to a boil. Reduce heat and simmer, uncovered, for 20 minutes, or until rice or pasta is tender. Stir in beans, zucchini and pepper; simmer for 5 minutes. Sprinkle with cheese before serving. Serves 5.

Sharon Ignash
Kinde, MI

Tomato-Basil Bisque

10-oz. can fire-roasted diced
   tomatoes with garlic
10¾-oz. can tomato soup

1 c. milk
3 T. pesto sauce

Mix together all ingredients in a saucepan over medium-low heat. Simmer until heated through. If desired, use an immersion blender to purée soup to desired consistency. Serves 4.

Stephanie Mayer
Portsmouth, VA

Such an easy, yummy way to dress up a can of tomato soup!

Pumpkin-Wild Rice Soup

1 T. butter
1 onion, diced
4 c. chicken broth
1 c. canned pumpkin

6-oz. pkg. long-grain & wild rice
   mix, cooked
½ c. whipping cream

Melt butter in a large saucepan over medium heat. Add onion; cook until softened. Stir in broth, pumpkin and prepared rice. Bring to a boil; reduce heat and add cream. Heat through, about 10 minutes. Serves 4.

Jennifer Martin
Manheim, PA

simple & delicious bread recipe

Bake a loaf of easy bread to go with your favorite soup. Stir together 3 cups self-rising flour, ½ cup sugar and a 12-ounce bottle of regular or non-alcoholic beer. Pour into a greased 9"x5" loaf pan. Bake at 350 degrees for 35 minutes. Drizzle 2 to 4 tablespoons melted butter over the loaf and return to oven for 10 minutes.

a welcome gift

Wrap up a soup-making kit for a friend...perfect for cold winter weather. Fill an enamelware soup kettle with a jar of Simmering Soup Bags, a package of small soup pasta, a ladle and a stack of hearty soup mugs.

Simmering Soup Bags

12 6-inch squares cheesecloth
¼ c. dried parsley
1 T. dried thyme

1 T. dried tarragon
12 bay leaves
kitchen string

On each cheesecloth square, place one teaspoon parsley, ¼ teaspoon thyme, ¼ teaspoon tarragon and one bay leaf. Tie into bags with kitchen string. Place bags in a large canning jar. Makes one gift jar of 12 bags.

Regina Wickline
Pebble Beach, CA

I make these flavorful packets with dried herbs from my garden. Sometimes I'll use mini cheesecloth bags from a kitchen supply store... just pop in the herbs and cinch the drawstring.

—Regina

Instructions: Add one bag to homemade vegetable soup, beef stew or spaghetti sauce during the last 30 minutes of cooking.

Soup mixes don't need to be layered in a jar if you're in a hurry. Spoon mixture into a plastic zipping bag, then place in a fabric gift bag or festive tin.

Patchwork Bean Soup Mix

½ c. dried kidney beans
½ c. dried blackeyed peas
½ c. dried black beans
½ c. dried red beans
½ c. dried split green peas
½ c. dried Great Northern beans
½ c. dried kidney beans
½ c. dried lima beans

¼ c. brown sugar, packed
3 T. chicken bouillon granules
1 T. dried, minced onion
1 T. dried parsley flakes
1 t. celery seed
½ t. garlic powder

Layer ½ cup of each type of bean in a one-quart, wide-mouth jar. In a plastic zipping bag, blend together sugar and seasonings. For gift-giving, attach instructions.

Regina Wickline
Pebble Beach, CA

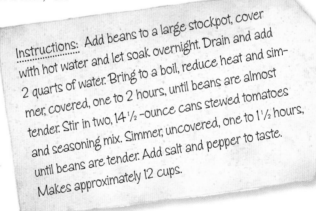

Instructions: Add beans to a large stockpot, cover with hot water and let soak overnight. Drain and add 2 quarts of water. Bring to a boil, reduce heat and simmer, covered, one to 2 hours, until beans are almost tender. Stir in two, 14½-ounce cans stewed tomatoes and seasoning mix. Simmer, uncovered, one to 1½ hours, until beans are tender. Add salt and pepper to taste. Makes approximately 12 cups.

patchwork
Bean Soup Mix

Place be
stockpo
water and s
night. Drain a
quarts of water
a boil over high
heat and simmer
1-2 hours or until
almost tender. St
14 ½ oz. cans stewe
atoes and seasonin
sim   uncovered
          bean

Tortilla
chips

Can of Diced
Tomatoes

A

Tortilla
Soup Mix

make a paper doll chain

Decorate a kid's tree with memories of their childhood. Take a piece of sturdy paper, about 16 inches long and five inches high. Pleat the paper strip into fanfolds about two inches wide. Fasten pleats together with paper clips at the top and bottom. Draw one half of a doll silhouette onto your paper. Using sharp scissors, cut out the shape. Make as many chains as desired and tape together. Spray paper dolls with gold paint or let the kids color them with crayons.

Tortilla Soup Mix in a Jar

¼ c. dried, minced onion
2 T. chicken bouillon granules
1 t. lemon pepper
1 t. dried cilantro
½ t. garlic powder
½ t. cumin
½ t. dried oregano

½ t. salt
1 c. long-grain rice, uncooked
2 to 2½ c. tortilla strips, coarsely crushed
10-oz. can diced tomatoes with chiles

Easy to make...flavorful and filling! Give Tortilla Soup Mix in a Jar with homemade salsa and a bag of chips to snack on while the soup's cooking.

Combine all ingredients except rice, tortilla strips and tomatoes in a bowl; set aside. Layer rice and seasoning mixture in a one-quart, wide-mouth jar. Fill paper bag or another jar with crushed tortilla strips. Tie jar mix to the can of diced tomatoes; attach instructions.

Regina Wickline
Pebble Beach, CA

Instructions: Place tortilla strips in a small bowl. Add rice and seasonings to a stockpot; pour in 10 cups water. Stir in tomatoes with chiles; bring to a boil. Reduce heat; simmer for 20 minutes. Spoon soup into bowls while hot; sprinkle with tortilla strips, if desired. Makes 3 quarts.

Celebration Cherry Bread Mix, page 147
Hickory-Smoked Popcorn Mix, page 150
Orange-Cranberry Marmalade, page 154

Easy Treats in a Twinkle

These super-easy mixes are fun to make and perfect for those last-minute gift ideas.

Chocolate Malt Cookies in a Jar

These tasty cookies will bring back memories of the soda counter at the local five-and-dime store!

2 ½ c. all-purpose flour
¾ c. malted milk powder
½ t. baking soda
½ t. salt

1 c. sugar
½ c. brown sugar, packed
2 c. semi-sweet chocolate chips

Combine flour, malted milk powder, baking soda and salt in a bowl, stirring to mix; spoon into a one-quart, wide-mouth jar and press firmly. Layer sugar, brown sugar and as many chocolate chips as will fit; press each layer firmly before adding the next and place any extra chocolate chips into a plastic zipping bag. Secure lid and attach instructions and, if needed, plastic zipping bag of extra chocolate chips.

Sally Swift
Jacksonville, FL

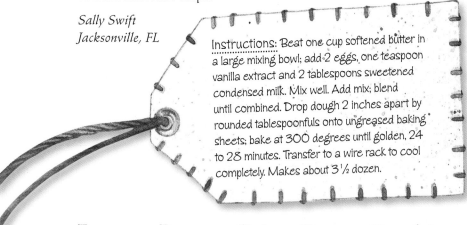

Instructions: Beat one cup softened butter in a large mixing bowl; add 2 eggs, one teaspoon vanilla extract and 2 tablespoons sweetened condensed milk. Mix well. Add mix; blend until combined. Drop dough 2 inches apart by rounded tablespoonfuls onto ungreased baking sheets; bake at 300 degrees until golden, 24 to 28 minutes. Transfer to a wire rack to cool completely. Makes about 3 ½ dozen.

Peanut Butter Criss-Cross Cookies in a Jar

Crunchy nuts, creamy peanut butter and chewy chocolate...the best combination.

1 ½ c. all-purpose flour
1 t. baking soda
½ t. salt
¾ c. mini chocolate chips

¾ c. chopped roasted peanuts
¾ c. brown sugar, packed
¾ c. sugar

Stir together flour, baking soda and salt. Layer chocolate chips, peanuts, flour mixture, brown sugar and sugar in a one-quart, wide-mouth jar; press firmly between additions. Secure lid and attach instructions.

Instructions: Empty cookie mix into a large mixing bowl; stir to combine. Add ½ cup softened butter, ½ cup creamy peanut butter, one beaten egg and 2 teaspoons vanilla extract; mix well. Drop by tablespoonfuls onto greased baking sheets; flatten slightly with tines of a fork. Bake at 350 degrees for 10 to 12 minutes. Cool for 5 minutes; remove to wire rack to cool completely. Makes about 3 dozen.

Tie on a whimsical cookie cutter along with the baking instructions for our Gingerbread Men Mix. Keep an eye out for vintage gingerbread-men shaped cutters at yard sales or antique stores.

Gingerbread Men Mix

3 ½ c. all-purpose flour, divided
1 t. baking powder
1 t. baking soda
1 c. brown sugar, packed

2 t. ground ginger
1 t. cinnamon
1 t. allspice

Sift together 2 cups flour, baking powder and baking soda. Spoon into a one-quart, wide-mouth jar, packing down tightly. Layer on brown sugar, pushing down well. Blend together remaining flour, ginger, cinnamon and allspice; layer over brown sugar and secure lid. Tie on instructions.

Instructions: Cream together ½ cup butter, ¾ cup molasses and one egg; blend in mix. Dough will be stiff. Cover and chill one hour. Roll out dough to ¼-inch thickness on a lightly floured surface, adding additional flour if dough appears too sticky. Cut out shapes with cookie cutters and place on lightly greased baking sheets. Bake at 350 degrees for 10 to 12 minutes. Makes 5 to 6 dozen.

S'mores in a Jar

1 sleeve graham crackers, crushed
⅓ c. brown sugar, packed

1 ½ c. mini marshmallows
1 c. milk chocolate chips

Layer ingredients in the order listed in a one-quart, wide-mouth jar. Secure lid; attach instructions.

Instructions: In a bowl, whisk together mix, melted butter and 2 tablespoons vanilla extract until well blended. Lightly pat mixture into a greased 9"x9" baking pan. Stir well; pat lightly into pan. Bake at 350 degrees for 15 minutes. Cool; cut into squares. Makes 16.

Give S'mores in a Jar along with some extra chocolate bars, marshmallows and graham crackers for toasting s'mores on a wintry day.

Gingerbread Brownie Mix

Gingerbread Brownie Mix

1 ½ c. all-purpose flour
1 c. sugar
¼ c. baking cocoa
1 t. allspice
1 t. cinnamon
½ t. baking soda
½ t. ground cloves

Combine all ingredients in a large mixing bowl; spoon into a plastic zipping bag. Attach instructions.

Instructions: Place mix in a medium mixing bowl; toss gently. Blend in ¼ cup melted butter, ⅓ cup molasses and 2 eggs. Spread into a greased 8"x8" baking pan; bake at 350 degrees for 20 minutes. Cool on a wire rack; cut into bars. Makes 2 dozen.

Celebration Cherry Bread Mix

pictured on page 142

2 ½ c. all-purpose flour
1 t. baking powder
1 t. baking soda
1 t. cinnamon
¼ t. nutmeg
½ t. salt
1 c. quick-cooking oats, uncooked
¾ c. dried cherries
¾ c. sweetened dried cranberries

Stir together flour, baking powder, baking soda, cinnamon, nutmeg and salt in a large mixing bowl; mix well. Add remaining ingredients; toss until blended. Place mixture in a plastic zipping bag or airtight container; attach instructions. Store in a cool, dry place.

Instructions: Whisk together ¾ cup honey, ¾ cup milk, ¾ cup melted butter and 2 beaten eggs; set aside. Place mix in a large mixing bowl; add honey mixture, stirring until just moistened. Pour batter into a greased 9"x5" loaf pan; bake at 350 degrees for 50 to 55 minutes, until a toothpick inserted in the center comes out clean. Cool on a wire rack. Serves 16.

Onion Bread Mix in a Jar

This recipe can also be baked in a bread machine; just follow the manufacturer's instructions for "white" bread.

¼ c. dried, minced onion
3 ⅓ c. bread flour
2 T. sugar
1 T. powdered milk
1 ½ t. salt
½ t. dried sage
1 env. active dry yeast

Place dried, minced onion in a small plastic zipping bag and set aside. Combine flour, sugar, powdered milk, salt and sage; spoon into a one-quart, wide-mouth jar. Tuck the plastic zipping bag and package of yeast on top; secure lid. Attach instructions.

Instructions: Sprinkle yeast over 1⅛ cups of 110- to 115-degree water; set aside until foamy. Place flour mixture in a large mixing bowl; add contents of plastic zipping bag. Blend in yeast mixture and one tablespoon olive oil; mix until smooth. Knead 5 minutes; place dough in a greased mixing bowl, turning once to coat both sides. Cover with plastic wrap and set aside to rise until double in bulk; punch down. Form dough into a loaf; place in a greased 9"x5" loaf pan. Cover and let rise until double. Bake at 450 degrees until golden, about 30 minutes. Makes 8 servings.

PB&J Muffin Mix

1 ½ c. all-purpose flour   2 t. baking powder
½ c. cornmeal   ½ t. salt
4 T. sugar

    Combine all ingredients; place in a plastic zipping bag. Arrange in a gift basket along with an 8-ounce jar creamy or chunky peanut butter and 6-ounce jar fruit jelly. Attach instructions.

Instructions: Add mix to a large mixing bowl; make a well in the center. In another bowl, mix ¾ cup peanut butter and 2 tablespoons honey together; blend in 2 eggs, beaten, and one cup milk. Pour into well; stir until just moistened. Fill greased muffin tins half full; place one teaspoon jelly in center. Add batter until ¾ full; bake at 375 degrees for 25 to 30 minutes. Makes one dozen.

Cowboy Cornbread Mix

3 c. all-purpose flour
3 c. cornmeal
1 ½ c. powdered milk

3 ½ T. baking powder
3 T. sugar
2 ½ t. salt

Blend all ingredients together; place in a tin or plastic zipping bag with instructions.

Instructions: Place cornbread mix in a mixing bowl; cut in ¾ cup shortening. Blend in 3 beaten eggs and 2 cups water; mix well. Spoon into a greased 9"x9" baking pan or cast-iron skillet and bake at 425 degrees for 15 to 20 minutes. Makes 12 to 16 servings.

howdy, cowboy!

For another easy gift-wrapping idea...pack up our Cowboy Cornbread Mix in a plastic zipping bag and wrap up in a bright red bandanna or set inside a cowboy hat!

Hickory-Smoked Popcorn Mix

pictured on page 143

4 qts. popped popcorn
2 c. mini pretzels
1 c. peanuts
⅓ c. butter, melted

1 t. hickory-smoked salt
½ t. seasoned salt
½ c. grated Parmesan cheese
½ c. bacon bits

Combine popcorn, pretzels and peanuts in a large mixing bowl; toss gently and set aside. Whisk together butter and salts; pour over popcorn mixture, stirring to coat. Sprinkle with cheese and bacon bits; serve warm. Serves 12.

Dorothy McConnell
Brooklyn, IA

National Little League Baseball Week begins the second Monday in June and the whole team will cheer when it comes to Buffalo Wing-Style Popcorn Mix!

Buffalo Wing-Style Popcorn Mix

2 ½ qts. popped popcorn, divided
2 c. corn chips, coarsely broken
1 c. dry-roasted peanuts
¼ c. butter

2 T. hot pepper sauce
1 t. celery seed
¼ t. garlic salt

Set aside 2 cups popcorn. Combine remaining popcorn, corn chips and peanuts in a large mixing bowl. Melt butter with hot pepper sauce, celery seed and garlic salt in a small saucepan over medium heat; pour over popcorn mixture, tossing to coat. Spread in an ungreased jelly-roll pan; bake at 350 degrees for 10 minutes. Place back into large mixing bowl; mix in reserved popcorn. Store in an airtight container. Makes about 12 cups.

Herb Rice Mix

4 c. long-cooking long-grain rice, uncooked
½ c. powdered milk
¼ c. dried, minced celery

2 T. dried parsley
2 T. dried thyme
1 T. dried marjoram
1 T. dried chives

Combine all ingredients; store in an airtight container for up to 4 months. Attach instructions. Makes 5 cups.

Instructions: Mix one cup mix with 2 cups chicken broth in a 2-quart saucepan; add one tablespoon butter. Bring to a rolling boil; reduce heat. Simmer, covered, until liquid is absorbed, about 10 to 15 minutes. Makes 4 servings.

Mollohan's Mix

Mollohan's Mix

½ c. dried apples, coarsely
    chopped
½ c. walnut pieces
½ c. dried pears, coarsely chopped

½ c. colorful, candy-coated
    chocolate mini baking bits
½ c. dried bananas

Looking for a treat for
the kids' teachers? A
jar of snack mix tucked
inside a red tin will be a
welcome gift.

    Combine apples, walnuts, pears, mini baking bits and bananas in order
listed in a one-pint, wide-mouth jar. Serves 4 to 6.

Pat Mollohan
Parkersburg, WV

celebrate...Italian style!

Fill a gift basket with a loaf of round bread, a bottle of garlic-olive oil and a jar of Bowl o' Bruschetta Blend. Toss in a classic Italian CD to really set the mood.

Instructions: Slice one loaf French bread baguette diagonally into half-inch to one-inch slices. Brush with olive oil; broil until golden. Place each circle on a serving dish; spoon Bruschetta Blend on top. Makes 10 servings.

Bowl o' Bruschetta Blend

1-lb. pkg. roma tomatoes, chopped and seeded
⅓ c. sweet onion, diced
¼ c. garlic, minced
¼ c. olive oil
2 T. fresh basil, chopped
¼ T. salt
¼ T. pepper

Combine all ingredients in a large mixing bowl; whisk well. Pour into an airtight container and refrigerate until giving. Attach instructions. Makes 2 to 3 cups.

Zippy Pepper Jelly

pictured on page 6

I use green or red bell peppers for Christmas jelly, yellow peppers for springtime and bright orange peppers for fall...they all taste great.

—Judy

5 c. sugar
⅓ c. red pepper, finely chopped
⅓ c. yellow pepper, finely chopped
⅓ c. orange pepper, finely chopped
½ c. jalapeño pepper, finely chopped
1 ½ c. cider vinegar
6-oz. pkg. liquid pectin
5 to 6 ½-pint canning jars and lids, sterilized

Combine sugar, peppers and vinegar in an 8 to 10-quart saucepan. Bring to a rolling boil over high heat; boil for 3 to 4 minutes. Remove from heat; let cool for 5 minutes. Add pectin, stirring constantly. Let mixture cool for 2 minutes, stirring to make sure pectin is mixed well. Pour into hot sterilized jars, leaving ¼-inch headspace. Wipe rims; secure with lids and rings. Process for 5 minutes in a boiling water bath; set jars on a towel to cool. Check for seals; attach instructions. Makes 5 to 6 jars.

Judy Awe
Lincoln, IL

Bowl o' Bruschetta
Blend

tie it on

Jars of jams and jellies look sweet with a shatterproof Christmas bulb. Use a paint pen to write names on colorful plump Christmas lightbulbs and secure around jar neck with a pipe cleaner.

Cranberry-Orange Chutney

An excellent relish for ham or turkey sandwiches...you'll definitely get requests for this one every year.

4 seedless oranges
½ c. orange juice
1 lb. fresh cranberries
2 c. sugar
¼ c. crystallized ginger, diced

½ t. hot pepper sauce
1 cinnamon stick
1 clove garlic, peeled
¾ t. curry powder
¾ c. golden raisins

Peel oranges and reserve the rind of 2 oranges. Thinly slice the reserved rind. Cut oranges into ¼-inch-thick slices and quarter. Combine orange rind and remaining ingredients except orange segments in a large saucepan over medium heat; reduce to simmer, stirring occasionally, until sugar dissolves and cranberries burst. Remove from heat; discard cinnamon stick and garlic clove. Add orange segments and toss together lightly. Cool completely. Pour into an airtight container and store in refrigerator. Makes 6 cups.

Orange-Cranberry Marmalade

pictured on page 143

My friends just love to receive gift jars of this easy-to-make marmalade! It's delicious on biscuits or homemade rolls, stirred into a bowl of hot oatmeal or even used as a glaze on a baked ham steak.

—Lois

32-oz. jar orange marmalade
12-oz. pkg. cranberries

5 to 6 ½-pint canning jars and lids, sterilized

Spoon marmalade into a microwave-safe 2-quart bowl. Coarsely chop cranberries in a food processor or blender; add to marmalade and mix well. Cover and microwave on high for 6 minutes; stir and cover again after 2 and 4 minutes. Spoon into hot sterilized jars, leaving ¼-inch headspace. Wipe rims; secure with lids and rings. Process in a boiling water bath for 10 minutes; set jars on a towel to cool. Check for seals. Store in refrigerator up to one year. Makes 5 to 6 jars.

Lois Bruce
Huntsville, AL

Peppermint Sauce

1 ½ c. peppermint candies, finely
    crushed

1 ½ c. whipping cream
7-oz. jar marshmallow creme

Combine all ingredients in a heavy saucepan; cook over medium heat until smooth and creamy, stirring constantly. Remove from heat; cool and store in an airtight container in refrigerator. Makes 2 ½ cups.

Stephanie Pulkownik
South Milwaukee, WI

Yummy on chocolate ice cream or blended into a milkshake.

Chocolate-Dipped Fruit

2 1-oz. sqs. semi-sweet chocolate
1 T. shortening

strawberries and grapes

Combine chocolate and shortening in a small saucepan over low heat; stir until melted. Remove from heat and cool slightly. Dip fruit in chocolate until partially coated. Place on a wax paper-lined wire rack and chill until set, about 15 minutes.

Leslie Stimel
Powell, OH

This dip is also delicious with mandarin oranges, bananas or kiwi.

Gingered Caramel Sauce

1-inch piece fresh ginger, sliced
1 c. whipping cream
1 ½ c. brown sugar, firmly
    packed

½ c. water
¼ c. butter
1 tsp. vanilla extract

Bring ginger and cream to a simmer in a large saucepan over medium heat, stirring occasionally. Remove from heat, and cool. In a separate saucepan, bring brown sugar and ½ cup water to a simmer over medium heat, stirring occasionally. Cover and increase heat to medium-high; cook 2 minutes. Uncover and cook, stirring occasionally, about 5 minutes, or until mixture is golden brown. Remove from heat. Stir in cream mixture, butter and vanilla. Cool. Store in an airtight container in refrigerator. Makes 2 cups.

Serve this yummy sauce over ice cream, pound cake or pumpkin pie. Be sure to tell the gift recipients to keep it refrigerated.

Metric Equivalents

The recipes that appear in this cookbook use the standard United States method for measuring liquid and dry or solid ingredients (teaspoons, tablespoons, and cups). The information on this chart is provided to help cooks outside the U.S. successfully use these recipes. All equivalents are approximate.

Metric Equivalents for Different Types of Ingredients

A standard cup measure of a dry or solid ingredient will vary in weight depending on the type of ingredient. A standard cup of liquid is the same volume for any type of liquid. Use the following chart when converting standard cup measures to grams (weight) or milliliters (volume).

Standard Cup	Fine Powder (ex. flour)	Grain (ex. rice)	Granular (ex. sugar)	Liquid Solids (ex. butter)	Liquid (ex. milk)
1	140 g	150 g	190 g	200 g	240 ml
¾	105 g	113 g	143 g	150 g	180 ml
⅔	93 g	100 g	125 g	133 g	160 ml
½	70 g	75 g	95 g	100 g	120 ml
⅓	47 g	50 g	63 g	67 g	80 ml
¼	35 g	38 g	48 g	50 g	60 ml
⅛	18 g	19 g	24 g	25 g	30 ml

Useful Equivalents for Liquid Ingredients by Volume

¼ tsp =				1 ml
½ tsp =				2 ml
1 tsp =				5 ml
3 tsp =	1 tbls	= ½ fl oz	=	15 ml
	= 2 tbls	= ⅛ cup	= 1 fl oz	=	30 ml
	= 4 tbls	= ¼ cup	= 2 fl oz	=	60 ml
	= 5⅓ tbls	= ⅓ cup	= 3 fl oz	=	80 ml
	= 8 tbls	= ½ cup	= 4 fl oz	=	120 ml
	=10⅔ tbls	= ⅔ cup	= 5 fl oz	=	160 ml
	= 12 tbls	= ¾ cup	= 6 fl oz	=	180 ml
	= 16 tbls	= 1 cup	= 8 fl oz	=	240 ml
	= 1 pt	= 2 cups	= 16 fl oz	=	480 ml
	= 1 qt	= 4 cups	= 32 fl oz	=	960 ml
			33 fl oz	= 1000 ml = 1 liter

Useful Equivalents for Dry Ingredients by Weight

(To convert ounces to grams, multiply the number of ounces by 30.)

1 oz	=	¹⁄₁₆ lb	=	30 g
4 oz	=	¼ lb	=	120 g
8 oz	=	½ lb	=	240 g
12 oz	=	¾ lb	=	360 g
16 oz	=	1 lb	=	480 g

Useful Equivalents for Length

(To convert inches to centimeters, multiply the number of inches by 2.5.)

1 in		=	2.5 cm
6 in	= ½ ft	=	15 cm
12 in	= 1 ft	=	30 cm
36 in	= 3 ft = 1 yd	=	90 cm
40 in		=	100 cm = 1 meter

Useful Equivalents for Cooking/Oven Temperatures

	Fahrenheit	Celsius	Gas Mark
Freeze Water	32° F	0° C	
Room Temperature	68° F	20° C	
Boil Water	212° F	100° C	
Bake	325° F	160° C	3
	350° F	180° C	4
	375° F	190° C	5
	400° F	200° C	6
	425° F	220° C	7
	450° F	230° C	8
Broil			Grill

Index

Beverages & Stirs

Apricot-Apple Cider, 106
Candy Tea Stirrers, 107
Chocolate Eggnog, 102
Christmas Snow Punch, 106
Creamy Cocoa 3 Ways, 102
Holiday Wassail, 106
Mocha Cocoa, 102
Nice & Spicy Cocoa, 102
The Sweetest Spoons, 107
White Hot Chocolate, 104

Breads, Biscuits & Muffins

Auntie Kay Kay's Sticky Buns, 119
Butter-Rum Muffins, 114
Chocolatey Banana Muffins, 117
Cranberry-Pecan-Coconut Loaf, 110
Cranberry Upside-Down Muffins, 114
Cream Biscuits, 123
Emma's Gingerbread Muffins, 115
Garlic Bubble Bread, 112
Golden Raisin Buns, 121
Holiday Eggnog Bread, 110
Marie's Yeast Rolls, 117
Mary's Sweet Corn Cake, 119
Mini Butterscotch Drop Scones, 123
Mini Cheddar Loaves, 113
One-Bowl Cheddar Biscuits, 122
Orange-Glazed Chocolate Rolls, 120
Rosemary & Onion Bread, 113
Simple & Delicious Bread Recipe, 135
Stone-Ground Corn Rolls, 118
Sunday Dinner Potato Rolls, 118
Velvet Pumpkin Bread, 112

Cakes

Chocolate Spice Cake, 91
Christmas Rainbow Cake, 78
Cranberry Swirl Cake, 85
Double-Chocolate Mousse Cake, 88
Eggnog Pound Cake, 84
Harvard Beet-Spice Cake, 87
Italian Cream Cake, 82
Sunny Lemon Cake, 85
Three-Layer Chocolate Cake, 81

Candies & Confections

Almond Brittle, 65
Bourbon Balls, 64
Cashew-Macadamia Crunch, 67
Chestnut Truffles, 69
Christmas Crunch, 74
Coffee Toffee, 74
Cookies & Cream Truffles, 64
Cranberry Poppers, 66
Creamy Butter Mints, 66
Double Chocolate-Orange Fudge, 62
Grandma's Peanut Brittle, 65
Maple Cream Candy, 70
Mocha-Pecan Fudge, 62
Mom's Peanut Butter Candy, 73
Pecan Turtles, 66
Peppermint Bark, 74
Puffy Marshmallow Cut-Outs, 73
Royal Coconut Creme, 70
Snowstorm Hard Candy, 71
Sparkling Sugarplums, 69

Condiments

Cranberry-Orange Chutney, 154
Orange-Cranberry Marmalade, 154

Zippy Pepper Jelly, 152

Cookies & Bars

Almond Cream Spritz, 21
Apple-Cheddar Bars, 48
Applesauce Spice Bars, 52
Blondies, 46
Brown Sugar Brownies, 47
Butterscotch Gingerbread Cookies, 29
Buttery Ricotta Cookies, 36
Cherry Cardamom Cookies, 27
Choco-Berry Goodie Bars, 53
Chocolate Crunch Brownies, 45
Chocolate-Mint Candy Brownies, 57
Christmas Peppermint & Chocolate Meringues, 39
Coconut-Pecan Fudge Bars, 56
Cool Mint Chocolate Swirls, 33
Corny Crunch Bars, 48
Dazzling Neapolitan Cookies, 18
Double-Dark Chocolate Brownies, 44
Espresso Bean Cookies, 22
Fruity Popcorn Bars, 58
Fudgy Cream Cheese Brownies, 44
German Apple Streusel Kuchen, 51
Ginger-Molasses Cookies, 30
Grandma Gray's Spice-Nut Bars, 51
Homemade Graham Crackers, 36
Key Lime Bites, 35
Lacy Florentine Cookies, 23
Maple Sugar Cookies, 24
Nellie's Persimmon Cookies, 30
Orangey-Ginger Cookie Sticks, 21
Peppermint Bark Brownies, 46
Powdered Sugar Sandies, 35
Quick Fruitcake Bites, 27
Red Velvet Brownies, 42
Rocky Road Crunch Bars, 54
Snowcap Cookies, 28
Sweet Raspberry-Oat Bars, 54

Teresa's Tasty Apricot Bars, 53
White Chocolate Cookies, 23

Desserts

Apple-Gingerbread Cobbler, 99
Chocolate-Dipped Fruit, 155

Frostings, Fillings & Toppings

Browned Butter Frosting, 52
Chocolate Topping, 88
Coconut Topping, 53
Cranberry Topping, 114
Cream Cheese Frosting, 42
Cream Cheese-Pecan Frosting, 82
Crumb Topping, 130
Fudge Frosting, 81
Gingered Caramel Sauce, 155
Glaze, 120
Peppermint Sauce, 155

Mixes

Bowl o' Bruschetta Blend, 152
Buffalo Wing-Style Popcorn Mix, 150
Buttermint Coffee Blend, 104
Celebration Cherry Bread Mix, 147
Chocolate Malt Cookies in a Jar, 144
Cowboy Cornbread Mix, 149
Gingerbread Brownie Mix, 147
Gingerbread Men Mix, 145
Herb Rice Mix, 150
Hickory-Smoked Popcorn Mix, 150
Mollohan's Mix, 151
Onion Bread Mix in a Jar, 147
Patchwork Bean Soup Mix, 138
PB&J Muffin Mix, 148
Peanut Butter Criss-Cross Cookies in a Jar, 144
Simmering Soup Bags, 137

S'mores in a Jar, 145
South Sea Tea Blend, 105
Tortilla Soup Mix in a Jar, 141

Pies

Caramel-Banana Pie, 95
Chocolate-Raspberry Cream Pie, 93
Eggnog Pie, 96
Maple-Pecan Pie, 92
Molasses Chiffon Pie, 94
Pear Pie, 95
Sour Cream-Apple Pie, 99
Sweet Potato Pie, 91
Turtle Pumpkin Pie, 92

Soups & Stews

Cauliflower-Cheddar Soup, 134
Chunky Minestrone, 134
Cider Mill Stew, 126
Crawfish-Corn Chowder, 132
Herbed Chicken-Barley Soup, 128
Holiday Best Oyster Stew, 132
Kielbasa-Cabbage Soup, 130
Pumpkin-Wild Rice Soup, 135
Roast Chicken-Corn Tortilla Soup, 128
Slow-Cooked Hearty Pork Stew, 130
Slow-Cooker Spicy Chili, 126
Tomato-Basil Bisque, 135
Tom Turkey Noodle Soup, 129
Turkey & Dressing Soup, 129

Project Index

Clothing & Accessories

Aprons, 15

Food Gift Packaging

Aluminum Cans, 15
Basket, 14
Brown Lunch Bags, 12
Burlap and Buttons, 12
CD Holders, 11
Coffee Mugs, 11
Ice-Cream Party Favors, 13
Supplies, 10
Tea Towels, 14
Wide-Mouth Jars, 13

Gift Tags, Cards & Wrap

Clothespin Gift Tag, 15
Felt Tag, 11
Tea Towel Wrap, 14
Valentine Tag, 11

Kitchen

Aprons, 15

Our Story

Back in 1984, we were next-door neighbors raising our families in the little town of Delaware, Ohio. Two moms with small children, we were looking for a way to do what we loved and stay home with the kids too. We had always shared a love of home cooking and making memories with family & friends and so, after many a conversation over the backyard fence, **Gooseberry Patch** was born.

We put together our first catalog at our kitchen tables, enlisting the help of our loved ones wherever we could. From that very first mailing, we found an immediate connection with many of our customers and it wasn't long before we began receiving letters, photos and recipes from these new friends. In 1992, we put together our very first cookbook, compiled from hundreds of these recipes and the rest, as they say, is history.

Hard to believe it's been over 25 years since those kitchen-table days! From that original little Gooseberry Patch family, we've grown to include an amazing group of creative folks who love cooking, decorating and creating as much as we do. Today, we're best known for our homestyle, family-friendly cookbooks, now recognized as national bestsellers.

One thing's for sure, we couldn't have done it without our friends all across the country. Each year, we're honored to turn thousands of your recipes into our collectible cookbooks. Our hope is that each book captures the stories and heart of all of you who have shared with us. Whether you've been with us since the beginning or are just discovering us, welcome to the **Gooseberry Patch** family!

We couldn't make our best-selling cookbooks without YOU!

Each of our books is filled with recipes from cooks just like you, gathered from kitchens all across the country.

Share your tried & true recipes with us on our website and you could be selected for an upcoming cookbook. If your recipe is included, you'll receive a FREE copy of the cookbook when it's published!

www.gooseberrypatch.com

We'd love to add YOU to our Circle of Friends!

Get free recipes, crafts, giveaways and so much more when you join our email club...join us online at all the spots below for even more goodies!